Angry Voices

Angry Voices

An Anthology of the
Off-Beat
New Egyptian Poets

Translated and with an introduction
by Mohamed Enani

Compiled by Mohamed Metwalli

THE UNIVERSITY OF ARKANSAS PRESS
FAYETTEVILLE
2003

Library of Congress Cataloging-in-Publication Data

Angry voices : an anthology of the off-beat : new Egyptian poets /
translated and with an introduction by Mohamed Enani ; compiled
by Mohamed Metwalli.
    p. cm.
    ISBN 1-55728-743-0 (paperback)
  1. Arabic poetry—Egypt—Translations into English. 2. Arabic
poetry—20th century—Translations into English. I. 'Inani,
Muhammad Muhammad, al-Duktūr. II. Mutawallī, Muhammad,
1970–

PJ8214.5.E5 A54 2003
892.7'1608--dc21

                                        2003000630

Acknowledgments

Grateful acknowledgment is made to the editors of the following magazines: *Fusul, Garad, Al-Qahirah,* and *Al-Kitaba el-Okhra,* in which a number of these poems first appeared, and to the poets; a number of these poems first appeared in their self-published collections. Grateful acknowledgment is also made to Ahmad Taha for his assistance with biographical information.

Grateful thanks are also due to Larry Malley for his unfailing belief in and devotion to this project, to editor Brian King, and to Sarah Enany for all her help. Last but not least, this book would not have been possible without the untiring efforts of Dr. Dalia el-Shayal, preliminary editor, facilitator, and liaison *extraordinaire.*

Contents

Introduction

Mohamed Enani

The voices in this collection are not "angry" in the sense of being enraged. Rather I have dubbed them "angry" in the sense of rebellion. In one way or another, each of these poets is rebelling against deeply entrenched customs—linguistic, metrical, formal, or social. The amount of anger that has been directed at these poets for "breaking" taboos and rules in our society is astounding. They stand, as it were, in the eye of a hurricane. Their main innovation is breaking with the established order. The notion of *order*, in fact, is at the heart of the matter.

If, as Morse Peckham says, art is there to liberate the world from "form," to give the ordered world a *"kind of disorder"* (*Man's Rage for Chaos: Biology, Behavior and the Arts,* New York: Schocken, 1969), then this is art par excellence. I have emphasized the above-quoted words because of their oblique reference to the title of the last volume by Stanley Kunitz—*A Kind of Order, A Kind of Folly*—which he presented to me personally when he visited Egypt, nearly twenty-five years ago. Kunitz was an old man, and we expected him to represent the mid-century modernism of the "Movement" poets in Britain or, if revolutionary, the calculated innovations of the "New" American poets—Ginsberg & co.; but he had a "deconstructive" streak in his thinking that upheld the new off-beat poetics, still inchoate, both in the English-speaking world and elsewhere. Our meeting, which took place in the apartment of the late Arabic poet Salah Abdul-Sabour, was anything but dull: he disapproved of all the Arabic poetry I had done into English, though I believed it had enough "disorder" to vindicate Baudelaire's dictum *"un peu désordre, c'est l'art."* Perhaps it is the *"un peu"* that disturbed him: he wanted poetry to break free totally of the order "imposed" on our vision by the tradition, to allow the poetic impulse to reign supreme and unbridled, so as to dictate "to the mind fresh modes of thought." To the Arab modernists taking part in the conversation, his words seemed "extremist." But I, though a reluctant modernist (not necessarily because of my Arabic classical upbringing) believed that he made a lot of sense. My trouble, in practice, was that I could never see how one could do in Arabic what others did in foreign languages. Arabic seemed to me to be a language that had to be peculiarly based on order: any departure from logic would destroy the structure of Arabic thought, hence of Arabic, and any innovations in style of the kind I admired, say in Dylan Thomas, would wreak havoc with the Arabic poem.

It was then that I discovered Peckham. Based on psychobiological data, and regarded as revolutionary in the heady years of the late 1960s, his theory came to coincide with the Chomskian doctrine about innate language capacity, the inborn ability to order ideas (and give them some sort of linguistic form) which confirmed the work of early twentieth-century language philosophers, and culminated in what Steven Pinker came to describe in *The Language Instinct* (1993). We are, in short, logical beings with in-built order; what applies to one language must apply to all others, and regardless of differences in "performance," the mind's "competence" must be seen as universal. Why should Arabic appear to be so different then? If the innermost principle is universal, Arabic should be no exception. The problem, I concluded, had little to do with Arabic as a language per se, and a good deal to do with our tradition.

It is a fact that the Arab mind is trained from the early stages of language acquisition to learn another mode of thought embodied in, and channeled through, an ancient (often archaic) variety of Arabic—commonly but inaccurately described as "classical" Arabic. The non-Arab reader may find it difficult to comprehend the dichotomy inherent in Arabic language acquisition. Language in most, if not all, Arab countries is divided into two types: spoken and written. There are significant differences between the two varieties. The first, or spoken variety, differs from country to country and is variously known as "colloquial Arabic," "vernacular," or "localized dialect." This variety differs from country to country and is in every sense of the word a "living" language, used in everyday life and in arts reflecting the spoken language of today, such as in films and plays. Using some of the vocabulary and some of the structures of "classical" Arabic, it nevertheless retains many elements of "local" structure and vocabulary that differ from the classical model; these also differ from country to country. The second, or written variety, usually known as "classical Arabic," has no local variants and, in its most traditional form (the form in which virtually all classical Arabic poetry is written), is regarded as the only language suitable for literary production. Coming to us directly from the ancients, with ready-made structures and vocabulary, it bears no relation to our everyday life, the more so because it comes with its own set of rhythms, phrases, and dead metaphors that pertain to the desert life of the ancient Arab world, as I shall explain below. Classical Arabic also exists in a less traditional, less rigid form, which I have identified and dubbed in my previous writings Modern Standard Arabic, or MSA for short. This language, used mainly by the press and news media but also by some creative writers as I shall discuss shortly, preserves the ancient structures and vocabulary—essential for any Serious written medium's credibility—but not the ancient idiom that makes "literary" classical Arabic so removed from our sensibility.

I stress the *"otherness"* of "literary" classical Arabic in spite of the many links that bind it, even intimately, with the modern standard variety used in writing and in the media, but never in thinking or conversation. A child is taught that "other" variety and is taught that his or her entire literary tradition is written in it. The introduction of Modern Standard Arabic has been gradual, as I have elsewhere explained in detail (*The Comparative Tone,* Cairo, 1995), and it has in time come to replace the ancient variety as the "language of literature." Compared with its antecedent, however, it is less rich in vocabulary, full of expressions borrowed (or naturalized) from European language, and vitally related to the vernacular (Egyptian Arabic).

To discuss how these varieties of Arabic are related would take me beyond my central argument, which is that there is a dichotomy made early in a child's education between the language which he or she speaks and in which he or she naturally thinks and the language he or she is taught as the language of literature. The sensibility of the young is therefore split between the living language, which is also the language of feeling, and the dead language which he or she is taught as the only one fit for literary production. A "good" student will "listen" and try to perfect his or her knowledge of archaic classical Arabic, an almost unattainable goal, and in the process will learn to impose the order of the defunct thought on the living world. His or her modes of thought will be controlled by those inherited from people who lived over a thousand years ago: and his or her models will be the poets who flourished in the eighth or ninth century A.D.

There have been attempts in every generation to revive those modes of thought through a revival of the language and techniques of verse that have existed, though with a checkered history, since the sixth century A.D., the most recent being that made by Mahmoud Sami Al-Baroudy, Ahmed Shawqi, Khalil Mutran, and Hafiz Ibrahim, who were "innovators" up to a point. These neo-classical poets belonged to the so-called "Revivalist" school which sought to return classical Arabic poetry to its former glory after the so-called Age of Decline, following the Abbassid era, when Arabic poetry languished. Consequently, they followed the ancient models; the classical, complex metrical structures; and most importantly, the ancient idiom (a detailed study of which follows). Their success was remarkable, but the people who enjoyed their verse diminished in number, as the teaching of classical Arabic in schools decreased and their "selections" were relegated to obscure corners of school anthologies.

The second wave of innovations, and innovators, fared better with the public. Salah Abdul-Sabour and Ahmed Abd el-Mo'ti Higazi were Egyptian pioneers of free verse, which simplified the complex structures of ancient Arabic and Revivalist poetry, taking the individual metrical unit, also known as a "foot" (Taf'ilah) as their structural element rather than the more compound versions used by the classicists. Using significantly more modern lexical items and concepts, these poets and others like them dealt with modern modes of thought, though they still flirted with the ancient idiom, each being an Arabic graduate, while the "old guard," the professors of Arabic, continued to write traditional verse that few people read.

Some thought that the solution to the problem—and it is a very real problem indeed—lay in writing in the vernacular. The living language was more capable, they thought, of transmitting their feelings and thoughts more directly—without the artificial mediation of the ancient idiom into which they had to translate their original feelings. Arabic professors had no problem: they had such a knowledge of ancient classical Arabic that they needed little effort in such translation or, sometimes, in feeling originally in classical Arabic.

Recourse to the vernacular (while preserving the freer metrical element of the *Taf'ilah*) was no doubt a solution, but it wasn't the only solution. In fact, it represented a parallel line, rather than a substitute. Sometimes the poets writing in the vernacular claimed to be drawing on folklore, representing the rich tradition of the people and their immediate concerns. Sometimes they claimed to be just poets writing in the real language of thought and feeling, much in the same way as Wordsworth and Coleridge did. Many opted for lyrics designed to be sung or included in musicals. And there were others who wrote in the vernacular because they felt classical Arabic was alien to them, and their detractors could only see this as an excuse for their ignorance.

The crisis persists. Apart from Arabic professors, as I have said, few people today write in the classical variety of Arabic, and their audience is definitely limited. It is perhaps only the poets themselves who may be tempted to read such poetry when published, even in a daily newspaper with a wide circulation. In the vernacular, the poem may stand a better chance of getting read, or heard. Poems in MSA are better received, especially if belonging to the kind I have described elsewhere as the "New Poetry," but the future of this "kind" is dim, and the poets are not encouraged by any promises of glory—much less of fame and fortune.

Today's situation can best be described as being characterized by a diversity of styles: we can find poets who still write in the ancient classical idiom, poets who write traditional verse using MSA, *Taf'ilah* poets using both MSA and the vernacular, and prose poets, who are represented in this volume. Virtually all the poets in this collection have rejected both the traditional metrical order and even the relative innovation of the *Taf'ilah* in favor of prose poetry. First pioneered in the 1950s, mainly in the critical writings (and, occasionally, the poetry) of Syrian *Taf'ilah* poet Ali

Ahmed Said (better known as "Adonis"), prose poetry steadily rose in popularity among the newer generations, reaching its peak in the 1980s and 1990s.

Not without its own rhythm, prose poetry is nonetheless frowned upon by the vast majority of critics. These new poets have rejected the old classical idiom to write in MSA, the vernacular, or a combination of the two. Prose poets, by and large, are not generally regarded as "real" poets, although things no doubt will change with time; for now, however, these writers remain underrecognized. Their collections are mainly self-published, their poems appearing in only a handful of magazines. With the significant exceptions of the state-published *Ibdaa'* (Creativity) and *Al-Qahirah* (Cairo), practically all of these are privately published with very little funds. The classically trained "old guard" and critical establishment refuse to accept these poets as anything more than an aberration. The crisis, as I have said, persists.

My own proposed diagnosis of the crisis rests on the Peckhamese idea of order versus disorder. Linguistic performance is only a reflection of the problem. To think in the old idiom is to impose an order, innate or acquired, on a world that is becoming increasingly disordered. When the modernists, led by T. S. Eliot, tried to do this, believing in the sense of "natural order" inherent in spiritual values, their efforts came to grief with the Second World War and the upheavals that followed. Larkin was the single most sincere modernist who captured the very real despair of a whole generation. Other "Movement" poets, in the typical pragmatic spirit of the British, have been variously cynical, flippant, sardonic, or, like Anthony Thwaite, genuinely sympathetic with the predicament of the helpless men and women who have to endure incomprehensible post-war compromises. In each case order has been imposed on disorder for the purpose of finding—or "in despair as not being able" to find—a meaning. The world has been changing in ways that only the rash could claim to be able to understand, and the Arab world, of which Egypt is a part, has proven to be enmeshed beyond everybody's expectations in the ongoing change. If the United States has its "Generation X," "baby boomers" and so forth, Egypt also has several generations who have lived through upheavals: First there is the "lost" generation, born around the 1960s and mostly in their forties now, who are old enough to have witnessed the collapse of President Nasser's pan-Arab idealistic vision and young enough not to have reaped any benefits from Sadat's open-door policy, the vast majority of whom are battling unemployment and struggling to find a niche for themselves at a relatively advanced age. Upheaval and an absence of "order" and security is the hallmark of their experience. The generation following them—many of whom make up the so-called "Nineties poets" movement—are now in their twenties and thirties. Growing up in the Mubarak era, characterized by materialism and an absence of idealism, these tend to be more cynical, more nihilistic, and more postmodern in the sense of rejecting the idea of Serious art and embracing an eclectic mix of cultural input. Faced with a world which is constantly changing, is it any wonder that they reject the established "order"?

Stanley Kunitz's poems do, by the way, advocate a "kind of order," though recognizing that it would be foolish to accept it as a norm. The Arabic modernists, from Salah Abdul-Sabour to Farooq Shooshah, Farooq Guwaidah, and Mahmoud al-Faytouri, believe in order—without qualification. Other major, and most popular poets, like Nizar Qabbani or Mahmoud Darwish, invariably reveal their belief in order. They are all in this sense romantics and idealists. The function of the poet to them differs little from that assigned to the poet by Shelley, Keats, Bisharah Al-Khouri, Elia Abu Madi, Ali Mahmoud Taha, Ibrahim Nagi, and the other explicitly romantic poets; all believe that a poet is a soul seeking perfection in order, attempting, even if against great odds, to read order in disorder. They all believe in the romantic ideal and, faced with disorder (in the form of social ills or otherwise), would fight to the bitter end, whether really to restore order or to simply imagine that it exists. Not so the group of poets who began writing in Arabic in the 1970s, who sought a clean break with tradition and believed that, order being an illusion, it would be fatuous to court it and that a real poet must grapple with disorder as "the order of the day."

The new evolution came, not unexpectedly, from the quarters of the young. Forty such poets were represented in my *Comparative Moments* (Cairo, 1996) with an introduction on their modernism or, occasionally, post-modernism. The modernists among them belonged, as I explained in the introduction, to the order-oriented camp; the present anthology, compiled by one of my former students, is more representative of the disorder-oriented group. Most are represented in this volume by poems which illustrate the real dimensions of their revolution. Their first target is rhythm: it is seen as an enemy because, more than any other quality, it stands for order. The hypnotic effect of rhythm is a major "device," they claim, in passing a kind of order to the reader. It is a trick, and it should be recognized as such from the outset.

The question of writing poetry not in verse but in prose seemed important enough to be discussed in a series of "academic bombardment" articles in the newspaper with the widest circulation in Egypt, perhaps in the Arab world as well—*Al-Ahram*. As the editor of the "Literary Page" is avowedly conservative, more views were published in rebuttal than in defense, and the conservatives seemed to have won the day. The arguments of each side were the old familiar ones about tradition, nomenclature, and taxonomy; few approached the argument for turning away from regular rhythm from the standpoint of the young poets themselves, now regarded as "huns," "vandals," or "locusts," the last being the name of one of the branches of their movement.

The young poets' argument, as approached from the point of view of "order," should not appear, in fact, too shocking. Rhythm, defined in terms of repeated phonological pulses, could be seen as more biological than emotional or psychological. Certain types of music, especially in the Orient, are rhythm-free; and many schools of modern painting have successfully opposed such regularity and symmetrical structures. "Tempo" has been redefined as "pace" rather than regularity; and the modern age in its entirety has been a manifestation of the anti-rhythmical progress of thoughts and feeling. The old argument of "similitude in dissimilitude"—that is, the recognition of an inner pattern of sound (a system of similarities) in a structure that holds together far from homogeneous material (unsystematic ideas, themes, and feelings)—is true of only one kind of poetry, or one kind of art. Humanity needs, they argue, other kinds, especially one that does not balance heterogeneity with an artificial phonological pattern.

The paradoxical possibility of producing a kind of poetry which is truly mimetic, by avoiding the imitation or the representation of the biological heartbeats in material that is far from biological, is therefore not precluded. Freedom from artificial rhythm of "sound" should, it is claimed, liberate the mind of the poet who seeks to imitate or represent only the "chaotic" patterns or forms of thought and feeling. The poetry produced will be thus different from any traditional verse which, they believe, is presented in prescribed or strictly defined phonological moulds. Theirs would be a different kind of poetry and as such could coexist in this age of relativity, or could somehow survive side by side with the traditional kinds of poetry written in verse.

Conscious that they were presenting another kind of poetry, contemporary prose poets describe their work as the "other poetry" (the name of another branch of their movement). At times it seemed an underground movement, insomuch at least as the "official" literary magazines published very little of it, sometimes in a condescending gesture. For some time only the poets themselves, with their numbers swelling daily, read this "other" kind; but more were attracted to the movement, and as some of them were cautiously accepted by the literary magazines and the editors of the "poetry book" series, their existence came to be recognized, though their work remains highly controversial.

An approach from the angle of "order," that is, from the Peckhamese viewpoint, should also explain these poets' opposition to rhyme, to logic, to cohesion, and, indeed, to coherence. But the opposition, apparently conscious and deliberate, has been in fact spontaneous and, to use a favorite word in romantic criticism, sincere. A modern poet seems, to the ordinary "order-oriented" reader, more like the "Waste Land" character who can "connect nothing with nothing"; he or she would even reject the cynicism of the modernists as it required a solid basis of truth or reality against which to measure any departure from it. The romantics, though professedly resisting any fixed social norms, still believed in deep-level human standards. And the modernists still aspired to those standards in their exasperation with the modern world. Now the post-modernists aspire to nothing: the literary exercise is sought as a single reflection of a world that has lost its bearings, a language that has more aporiae than referents and "signi-fieds," and a human psyche that is denied being a subject, but is regarded as a focus or a conjuncture of ever-changing historical and social forces.

The rejection of the above-mentioned features of traditional verse must therefore be seen as a rejection of meaning, defined in terms of the traditional assumptions or pre-suppositions about the world inherent in the inherited order. How gratifying, con-temporary poets will argue, it is for the reader to reach the rhyme word at the end of the line; it is a gratification that is confirmed by the reverse—the absence of the word. The gratification is to a certain extent part of the traditional "poetic" meaning: the reader, as I. A. Richards intimated (and experimentally proved), and as Stanley Fish confirmed, and as Wolfgang Iser formally for-mulated, participates in the production of such meaning. To manipulate the text in such a way as to deny the reader any ful-fillment of expectation may do more than infuriate him or her, it may simply tell the reader that his or her assumptions may or should be called in question. The poet may be aiming at shaking the very foundations upon which the reader's knowledge of the world is based and, by bringing epistemological questions into play, may be asking the reader indirectly to reconsider the logic inherent in language.

Here we reach the core of the new experiment, which has been quickly glimpsed at in the early part of this introduction. Questions of coherence are traditionally regarded as purely lin-guistic, and semantic theory still aspires to a formalization relat-ing meaning to structure (syntax or grammar). The use of Egyptian Arabic was, I have suggested, one way of averting the falsification of using the dead idiom inherited from ancient clas-sical Arabic; but not everybody would use the living language and risk being classified with the vernacular poets who could not, or possibly would not, write verse in MSA and who are thus excluded from the official list of poets.

Many young men and women, perhaps instinctively, realized that there was an inherent order representing essential con-straints on free or original thinking and feeling. MSA is inti-mately related, as I have said, to the ancient variety of Arabic and is characterized by many of its "cognitive" features. Arabic linguists and semanticians have explained the survival of ancient logic, and Aristotelian rules, in ancient Arabic; and it has been shown, more recently, that Arabic grammar in use today evolved with reference to ancient Greek philosophy. To sound truly Arabic, a text must relate to the categories of the ancients, must reflect the steady, unhurried movement of syntax, and the almost peremptory suppositions that ruled the ancient world. The poetic tradition of our forefathers has come to be the storehouse of all the modes of thought (and idiomatic Arabic) established by the ancients. The prose that survives, in the speeches and homilies of Ali Ibn-Abi Talib or in the epistles of Abi Al-Alaa Al-Ma'arri genuinely reflects the world picture that existed in the Middle Ages. The problem with MSA therefore was how completely it could break the fetters of the ancient logic and introduce a mode of thought or feeling more pertinent to the logic of the modern world.

A way out seemed to be available in the translations of foreign poetry, done mostly in prose, that appeared liberated enough from such an ancient logic. Reflecting a different but modern culture, these translations had all the features of the contemporary logic associated with the modern world. However careful the translator is, there will always be a "thought core," hence a linguistic pattern, pertaining to English, French, or German. There was something, too, in what I have described in previous writings (such as *The Comparative Tone,* Cairo, 1998) as "translation style," that appealed to the young poets—namely the tendency to precise definition, the ability to interrupt and resume syntax, and, most important of all, the utter rejection of ancient poetic diction. To appreciate the real dimensions of such a revolution as this volume represents, one may need go no farther afield than compare the work of these young people—especially their style—with classical Arabic styles.

The reader has so far been referred to the other studies I have contributed to translation scholarship, but I subscribe to the view that such references are the "lazy writer's way out." Examples will therefore be given to illustrate the fact that the idiom of classical Arabic, both the ancient variety and MSA, even when regarded as the finest and most elevated, reflects modes of thought that the modern world may find hard to accommodate.

An immediate example is the common formula بأبي أنت و أمي —sometimes thought to be an oath and translated as "By my father and my mother." (The literal rendering is "By my father you are and my mother.") It is not, in fact, an oath at all but an exclamation expressing either great admiration or deep loyalty; it is an elliptical version of أفديك بأبي و أمي that is "I would give both my father and my mother in ransom to have you freed from captivity" or "I'd sacrifice both father and mother to save you." (The preposition ب here does not mean "by," but "worth," signifying price or value. Today we might say in MSA الرداء بعشرة جنيهات —"the garment costs/is worth ten pounds.") The formula with its underlying idea of "ransom" is obviously rooted in the traditions of the warring Arab tribes from time immemorial. The meaning of the original version is preserved in such books of antiquity as the Prophet's Biography (قال بأبي أنت و أمي يا رسول الله) ("He said 'You are [worthy to be ransomed] by my father and my mother, O Messenger of God.'") and has been modified to suit present-day purposes by the revivalist poets (those who, at the start of the twentieth century, led a revival of the ancient Arabic poetic style, meter and language in their writing), led by "Prince of Poets" Ahmed Shawqi, though the meaning has been confined to that of admiration. Consider Shawqi's

بأبي وروحي الناعمات الغيدا   الباسمات عن اليتيم نضيدا

The first hemistich means "I would give my father and soul as ransom/sacrifice, to [save] those beauties brought up in the lap of luxury." The same meaning may be found in Shawqi's heir to the throne of modern poetry, Bisharah Al-Khouri:

أسقنيها بأبي و أمي   (لا تجلو الهم عنى أنت همي)

The first hemistich means: "Oh, give me that cup to drink! I would sacrifice/give as ransom both father and mother! [to save] you."

The idea of sacrifice/ransom is sometimes spelled out and is, in fact, unequivocal:

أفديه إن حفظ الهوى أو ضيعا (ملك الفؤاد فما عسى أن أصنعا)

And the first hemistich: "I would sacrifice/give as ransom myself [to save] him, whether he keeps the bond of love or breaks it."

The idea of ransom is so essential to any understanding of the culture of the ancient Arabs that to ignore it is to misconstrue much of our linguistic tradition. A prisoner of war, if of a high rank in the tribe, would automatically be exchanged for a peer or for a huge sum of money. As a statement of great esteem for the captive, his people would claim to be willing to offer their best—even their nearest and dearest:

أفديه بالنفس لا بالمال ان عثرت (به الرحال و صال الدهر أو غدرا)

The first hemistich: "I would sacrifice/give as ransom my soul rather than my money if he was thrown off the back of the camel" etc.

The idea of sacrifice itself is deeply rooted in our tradition—from the pre-Islamic days of pagan "offerings" to the Islamic "Feast of Sacrifice" which commemorates the sacrifice of Abraham who on God's orders was about to kill his own son, but, according to the Quran, a "ransom" was sent from heaven to save the boy (و فديناه بذبح عظيم). Today's *fedayeen* are those who "sacrifice" (*ifdi*) or are willing to sacrifice themselves for a noble cause.

It is therefore common to come across the word and its cognates in contexts not at all meaning literal ransom or sacrifice. *A poet using this formula is therefore invoking a mode of thought alien to the modern world.* Consider the following instances from Shawqi:

أغير ليلاى نادوا أم بها هتفوا   فداء ليلى الليالي الخرد الغيد

"Did they call another Leila or mine own? For Leila's sake may be sacrificed/given in ransom such lovely and beautiful nights!"

قولوا له روحي فداه   هذا التجني ما مداه

"Oh, will you ask him—for whom I could give away (in sacrifice/ ransom) my life—'How long will he be so unfair?'"

A reader not used to the typical Arabic idiom may be puzzled by the reference to the beloved as "he" when in fact it should be "she." Feminists may be annoyed to hear that this was one way of "enhancing" the status of the beloved; but this is, in fact, only partly true. The masculine pronoun was used in classical Arabic to save the poet from mentioning the name of his beloved, as this would mar her reputation and hence was considered socially reprehensible. It was, in other words, a means of overcoming the "gender problem"—a kind of unisex fashion. The converse was the giving of feminine names to males, a phenomenon variously interpreted, though it is thought that it had origins in all Semitic languages. If a man's name is, say, Waraqa, meaning "a paper," and the word for paper happens to be feminine in Arabic (with a lexical gap for the masculine) then his name will sound feminine, such as حماسة (Hamasa). If he is to be given an abstract name— and all or most abstractions are feminine, then his name will sound feminine such as شناعة (in fact a famous Iraqi petroleum expert is called شناعة [Shana'a]). Abstractions are used as names for both sexes such as نهاد (Nehad) and (عصمة) عصمت (Esmat). Certain things to which a girl is compared in traditional Arabic verse are masculine (القمر + الغزال) (a gazelle and the moon, etc.) which may be another reason for the change in pronoun:

مثل الغزال نظرة و لفتة   من ذا رآه ماشيا و لا افتتن

"Like a gazelle is he in the way he looks, and the way he turns his head! No one could have watched him walking without being charmed."

أمانا أيها القمر المطل   ففي جفنيك أسياف تسل

"Assure me of safety, O moon now looking down [from the sky]! Your eyelids are sheaths whence swords are now drawn!"

The opening word of the above-quoted line is a glaring example of the linguistic formulas reflecting modes of thought. I have rendered it here as "safety" (with a suggestion of "safe passage") but the common modern meaning is "feeling of security" or even "peace." These three words form a configuration directly attributable to ancient Arab customs. The life of the Arabs in the desert was fraught with dangers of all sorts. Now the word "peace," which has come to mean a greeting, had its origin in asking for a "safe passage" and "security of person." The origin is purely historical. In pre-Islamic days, if a group of Arabs in the desert heard approaching horsemen or noticed a rising cloud of dust in the distance, their immediate reaction was to draw their swords. The riders could be highwaymen or members of an invading tribe. Hence the need for "peace be upon you" as a declaration of "good will," and hence the greeting. The Arabic word for peace covers the members of the "semantic configuration," that is الأمن (security) الأمان (feeling of security) and السلامة (safety). The verb يؤمن means to reassure someone of his or her safety and of the speaker's peaceful intentions; hence يعطي الأمان. The same verb is used in some Arab countries today as a loose equivalent of "ensure," and even to "insure" and "assure"—hence "insurance" and "assurance" in the economic senses. But such modern implications are totally absent from Shawqi's verse, though he is a poet of the twentieth century:

قف تمهل و خذ أمانا لقلبي   من عيون المها و راء السواد

"Stop, or gently pass, but see that I shall be safe from the arrows shot at my heart by the eyes of the deer beyond the grove."

Rendered as "deer," the Arabic word is said to mean a she-bison (a cow?). Again, the tradition has forced Shawqi to say things which he could not have wanted to say, about things he could not have seen.

Such is the power of the tradition, in fact, that a writer cannot hope to sound genuinely Arabic without invoking the literary tradition, and with it the traditional modes of thought. Some of these are easy to trace to particular works or sources, but the majority belong to the common Arabic legacy. An easy one, again from Shawqi, is a line from his famous خدعوها بقولهم حسناء "They Deceived Her by Calling Her Beautiful":

أنتم الناس أيها الشعراء نازعتني ثوبي العصى وقالت

"She pulled at my immaculate garb saying 'You are the real men, O poets!'"

The obvious reference is to Joseph, the Patriarch, and Potiphar's wife—the wife of the Egyptian king (chief of the guard, according to the Bible). As told in the Quran, the sinful woman tried to "have" Joseph and pulled so hard at his garb that she tore it from behind, while he tried to get out of the room (و استبقا الباب و قدت قميصه من دبر - ١٢:٢٥)

But the literary source is the line by Bashar Ibn Bourd:

برد الشباب و قد طويته   جاءت إلي تسومني

"She came to me to seek the garb of youth, which I had already folded up"—a line of exceptional beauty, especially with the "sunken image" at the end, which again refers to a verse from the Quran that involves folding and unfolding life: on the last day, the heavens will be folded up, only to be unfolded again! (Quran, The Prophets 21:104)

(يوم نطوي السماء كطي السجل للكتب، كما بدأنا أول خلق نعيده)

Such is the richness of the long cumulative tradition.

Intertextuality seems in fact to be such an essential feature of classical Arabic (mostly classical but also MSA) that the reader is required to be knowledgeable, up to a point, of the tradition. When in idiomatic Arabic we say فلان لا تلين قناته or فلان لا تلين له قناة the reader should, even without knowing what the precise meaning of قناة is, guess the general sense, namely that someone is unwaveringly firm/strong. But a poet may be addressing a different reader—one who knows that it is a piece of wood which, together with a blade, becomes a spear. A synecdoche for a spear, it occurs in Al-Mutanabbi:

ركب المرء في القناة سنانا   كلما أنبت الزمان قناة

"Whenever time produces the wooden handle of the spear [from the earth] man fixes a blade to it."

And Shawqi plays with the metaphor:

ولن نرتضي أن تقد القناة   و يبتر من مصر سوادنها

"We will not accept that the spear be broken, And Egypt be deprived of her Sudan."

In short, in contrast to the neo-classicists/Revivalists, our contemporary young poets do not require their readers to be conversant at all with the tradition. Intent on liberating their minds from the tradition of Arabic, they attempt a style reflecting the mode of thought which appears to fit a "thoughtless" world. But they cannot escape another tradition, namely that of the New World Order, which seems to be foisted on a whole generation. Some seek a way out in "regression": the anthology is full of fathers and mothers and childhood themes; some focus on sex, though with a strange disregard for the meaning of sex as traditionally held; others are solipsistic, self-involved and, as though puzzled by the problem of identity in a world that has changed beyond all recognition, wage an apparently losing war for the recovery of their vision—clear and unblurred.

But in rejecting the Arab tradition, with a few exceptions, they have substituted another. The substitute is foreign, without belonging to any specific foreign culture or tradition. The translation style is symptomatic of their attempt to get behind classical Arabic idiom to a neutral world. Their foreign idiom (dancing, dolls, cameras, etc.) is universal enough to fit even in the Egyptian culture; but the modes of statement are deliberately anti-Arabic. As I have decided not to go into detail about the poems, I shall not give examples from particular poems nor pass judgements on any of them. But reading them yet again, in their English version, I have felt that a handful showed great talent, and that whether the poets are reconciled or not to the Arabic tradition—at least to rhythm, if not to rhyme as well—they hold the promise of a real revival of poetry in Egypt and the Arab world. However, translation style, I must admit, still bothers me.

When a friend of mine observed that one of the poems in this anthology "seems to have been translated or copied from somewhere," I thought he was not far wrong. "Seems" is definitely the right word; and the poet wanted his or her work to "seem" so. But, if translated, he might have added, the text does not give credit to the translator, for, rather than give the cultural equivalent, he or she sticks to the culture of the putative original text. In fact, many poems in this volume appear to qualify for this description. You'll look in vain for the clichés of classical Arabic, for the idiom of the archaic language, or even for the inherent logic that has sustained our tradition. But you will encounter foreign names, "foreign" ideas, and even "foreign" structures, with a hint, just a hint, of intertextuality. Too much of that would defeat the purpose of the new poetic experiment.

But the poems may not be written off as pale imitations of original European models: the virtuosity of so many young people in attempting such fresh structures is amazing. They are not all of the same caliber, of course, but the better ones reveal a perfect command of form, or anti-form, and a rare ability to shock the reader. In their attempt to defy traditional logic, some have verged on the absurd. Their major predecessor is Eugene Ionesco, Beckett, or Genet. The sudden transitions are made not in the modernist tongue-in-cheek manner but in the earnest vein of people who take life seriously. If there is such a thing as "poetry of the absurd," here are many examples of it.

One may conclude from this account of the new poets that their work has focused on questions of language and form. True, these questions occupy a prominent place in their practice (and theory) but these are more consequences than motives for their poetic experiment.

The motive has been said to be none other than the classical ideal of representing genuine human experience in some sort of verbal art form. Modernism has been repeatedly defined as a movement opposed to the ideal of representation which is based on a realist impulse: all the schools of modernism in art—first in painting, then in literature and music—have shunned the "imitation" of nature (or its representation) in the belief that it could only mean "slavish" dependence on external reality and have sought sources of inspiration capable of liberating the mind from its traditional role as "a poor pensioner on outward forms," as Wordsworth put it.

Turning to inner vision, the "modernists" sought to "create" a new reality—as though to capture in their work "the light that never was on sea or land" (to cite Wordsworth again). Wasn't that what Blake did, or tried to do in his "prophetic" books and in *Milton*, with the strange color engravings accompanying that strange poem? Abundant instances of earlier attempts to get behind outward forms, including the "semantic substance" of words, as Vygotsky calls it, in search of hidden meanings and perhaps more "vital" symbols, have shown that they are fraught with the danger of esotericism.

There is a limit beyond which any total reliance on inner vision can lead to incomprehensibility, as is true of many poems in this volume. For a poet to be understood, a certain "common ground" with the reader should be established; "common codes" need to be used to ensure that the poet is initially accepted. This may save him or her from being too vague, too incoherent, or even inarticulate by being completely immersed in an inner vision and utterly consumed by it. A balance should, it has been argued, be maintained between the inner and the outer, the private and the public, for the reader to succeed in perceiving the "new" reality thus "created." It is only through the common that the special can be seen, but these young men and women have been less concerned about comprehensibility than about finding a "cooperative reader," more about the truthfulness of their experiences than about the potential response of the "receiver." They are out to shock, to surprise, and to alert their readers to untenable realities, even to a questionable "poetic" reality.

It may be too early to assess the extent of their success, for they as a group have lived up to their ideal of opposition to order. And opposition to order in a world already suffering from the disruption of many kinds of order is hazardous. Still, as the representative samples will abundantly show, every kind of poetic form and anti-form will be found: the short, crisp poem, the long rambling tale, the rigmarole, the mumbo-jumbo, the carefully planned illogico-logico-philosophico-poem, the fantastic vagary, the expressionistic picture with revolting and utterly disgusting details, but more importantly, the poems in the vernacular, and those in verse!

It will be the task of the reader, rather than the critic, to decide which kind is more capable of surviving. But survival belongs to the future, to a world I am not likely to see, and my concern is with the present. That these poets are a peculiar phenomenon of the 1990s is a fact that the literary historian must record; I have delayed my recognition of it to the last minute, perhaps wondering if it would just "go away," but it is very much with us today, and I could not, regardless of my personal predilections, put off my duty any longer.

As a translator I have strenuously endeavored to present the poems in levels of language that I believe to be the exact equivalents of the original Arabic. I have not interfered in any way— never suppressing a word, a statement or an idea, never adding anything, however insignificant, to the text. Mine has been a kind of documentary translation, with the focus consistently on the source text, not the target text. As I have done in my previous translations of poetry, I made a point of securing the approval of many of the poets themselves (regarding their English versions). Sanctioned by the authors, any changes must be seen as original rather than reflections "dimmed by the mirror of the translator's mind." Problems of interpretation have sometimes been insuperable; but, in the case of ambivalence or ambiguity, the poet's opinion has helped my choice.

As a critic I must suspend my own judgment, particularly in such a brief introductory note as this: my purpose has been to establish the critical framework for the "experiment," not to evaluate it. I already feel a stranger in the world of the young, and owing to my firm faith in time and change, I am confident that these young poets (some of them at least) will develop into great poets—the great poets of the future that I shall never see.

M. Enani
Cairo, 2003

Angry Voices

Zahrah Youssri

A graduate of Cairo's Ain Shams University's Faculty of Arts in 1995, Zahrah Youssri first published her poems in such official periodicals as *Al-Qahirah* (Cairo) magazine and such unofficial ones as *Al-Khitab al-Hamishy* (Marginal discourse) and *Al-Kitaba al-Okhra* (Other writings). Her first collection, *Zugag Yatakassar* (Breaking glass) was published by Al-Kitaba al-Okhra Books in 1996.

Why Are Seamen Always Miserable?

"Things are as usual mute"
A statement scribbled by an amateurish girl on an "introduction card"; and, without an appointment, put off by me, I shall cause those things to speak and move, over your heads. As is your wont, you shall peep through the keyhole to watch me as I talk to them, counting the tile squares, waiting.

I do not know precisely whether I shall kill you all horribly in my dreams or cause you to die an easy death, without visualizing with me the boy who urinates blood in a fountain that once was of bright white marble.

Am I so aggressive?

Or are the seamen now catching roast fish, without "realizing that I still whisper to the oysters imaginary things—wishes" wrapped in unusual spirituality?

Perhaps I now conceal my fear behind strident tones, but I will definitely practice the hate I lately learned, so that my belly will be swollen, bearing an imaginary baby, which will soon come out into the world, with an ugly face and fierce dreams.

Inevitably you will believe me when I say that the wolves gathered round me as I slept on the grass, resting my head on my arm, that the moon shone bright in their eyes when, one after another, they came and kissed me good night. And—but please don't laugh at me—the breath of the wolves on my face felt so soft that I fell into deep sleep, dreamed of mute things fondling me and of my sweetheart who suddenly changed into a horse running with me on the shore of a sea strewn with the skeletons of primitive people who woke up at night to cover me with quilts of soft straw.

Surely—

The school bag was full of memories which now seem insignificant. They will therefore stir no feeling of regret in me when I bid my sweetheart farewell on a dirty platform hardly fit for a final embrace. I shall tell him that lovers' conversations die, leaving nothing behind apart from the insipid daily habits and a very wide smile flowing on the lips.

—Of course that was not the story of the miserable seamen. This is entirely different.

It is as though the sun always went down at that time.

I stood on top of an old lighthouse (it is not important that it should be historical) what is important is that I saw the seamen pulling out their nets, full of bloated dead bodies. Their women will not, however, wait for too long, but will turn into pirates who will capture the men, hang them naked, having plucked out their moustaches and castrated their young boys. True, they will be wearing black eye-patches and adorn themselves with skulls and bones, but they are in fact very kind. Having chopped up the bodies of their husbands, they used the organs in making charms, decorated with sacred rings, with inscriptions—letters that belong to older times. So old in fact that the rings, as I remove them, turn into dust, while the highly strung organs begin to relax completely.

As for me, yet again, well—

It is as though the lighthouse sank with me to the bottom of a stagnant sea, with the stench surrounding me on all sides.

Why do I imagine then that a miserable girl could with her weeping wake up the dead? For the dead are dead; they will not be conscious of a solitary girl who envies the sleeping folk and curses all books and papers?

I shall therefore leave the pirate women and the dead alone, but will rather invite my sweetheart to watch a thriller—a bloody film—where the heroes die before the action starts, but which ends as usual with a victory for the good guys.

So, endings are always happy!

But my end will be totally different. This does not mean that it will be tragic. On the contrary, I shall indifferently put an end to everything.

I shall walk, like the night, unpoetically—without such faded shadows as appear behind the closed window—always alone, unawed and intrepid. This time I shall not look for someone who professionally masquerades behind my miserable need.

Only—

I shall make do with my sad tune with which I shall disturb the sleeping people.

I shall linger under their windows and sing in a rough voice that does not at all accord with the mood of the sad words.

I may push my wheelchair forward, rushing among the speeding cars to force people to scream, and the savage children will have to sympathize with the solitary girl who tries to hurt all others.

August 1996

Mohab Nasr

Alexandrine by birth, Nasr is classified by critics as an "Eighties poet," i.e., belonging to the intermediate stage between 1970s pioneers of prose poetry, such as Adonis, and the latest wave of 1990s poetry. A poet, translator, and critic, he is a member of the editorial board of numerous magazines, including *Amkena* (Places). He is a member of the editorial board of *Al-Arba'a'eyoun* (The Wednesdayers), an independent Alexandrine magazine that deals with different places, their history, and character.

"_____"

With meek eyes
She stood before the birds' cage
But asked the shopkeeper for a dog.
She was very lonely
And wanted to buy a dog.
The shopkeeper fully reviewed his dogs:
There was the book reader,
The saint,
The merry lame
Casanova—that was his name.
There was finally the "devil."
The woman hung her head, disappointed;
The dog made feline purrs, then barked
And sallied forth at the cats.
A dog with which to spend a weekend,
When he and she looked
At each other's loneliness,
Unaware of the secret of this sympathy.
More importantly, a dog that reminded her

Of no one she knew.
The shop keeper was enthusiastic for the idea,
Nodding, appearing to see the dog
In his mind's eye, but making no progress:
How could he make a promise to her?
He spoke in discreet syllables
My . . . La . . . dy
And waved his hand
As though he could not know
That he himself may have low-hanging ears
And a love-elongated skull,
Or that "His Excellency" could have a tail
Which he might wag to welcome all visitors!
What a difficult condition!
How could he guarantee her
That it will be a real dog
Without reminding her of someone she knows?

1993

Mahmoud Sharaf

Sharaf graduated from Tanta University's Faculty of Arts in the province of Tanta in 1996 and has published his poetry in *Al-Qahirah* (Cairo) and *Al-Kitaba al-Okhra* (Other writings) magazines. He currently works as a teacher. His first collection, *Howwat Tabi'eya* (Natural mistakes) was self-published in 1997.

Dali

Suddenly I find out that my fingers
Are larger than a good rose,
That I have become incapable
Of making a geometric design,
Not even of paper,
Fit to receive three children
Whose cheeks might blush
When I kiss their mother before them.
I find out, too, that I have not understood
Gala completely:
More parts are revealed to me of that soul
That lies down on her stomach
Like a little cat
Playing about with wonderful rhino horns
And the threads of canvases tightly woven,
Between the knees of a short woman,
Where the thread reaches down over her knee,
And ends with the cat.
The streamlined brightness within
Allows no more scenes than the memory holds.
It is the end that I had expected,
For the cat is now entirely entangled

In the thread—nothing much remains.
I shall imagine a light pillow
That no longer attracts flies
And a transparent body that went out
Of the window and never came back.
I have no need now for the three children
For my organs have become more flaccid
Than a good rose that slowly dies out now,
And the little cat can do nothing more now
Than lie down on her belly
To get herself more bright scenes to watch.

August 1996

Behind the House

The thorn that grew in her coat,
Preventing her from moving easily,
And from climbing up the trees
As was her wont,
Was natural—a natural, respectable thorn
Like those big headlines in the newspapers
That I use in wrapping up
Those *Ta'miyah** sandwiches which I love.
She moved about like an old cat
Concealing her endemic anxiety within
Towards the lemon trees behind the house.
She believes that she resembles
an oyster shell,
though the oyster be dead inside,

---

*Egyptian name for the fried balls of bean paste more commonly known
as *falafel* in Arab countries such as Lebanon, Syria, and Iraq.

But she doesn't want to show it to me.
Oh, calm down now,
No one will force you to abandon
Your transparent body.
Calm down and light your cigarettes
As slowly as you wish,
As slowly as a cat that has not
Finished the licking of her body
Under the bright sun.
Dead thorns are less fierce
Than the *Ta'miyah* headlines.

July 1996

Ahmed Taha

Taha is one of the most important figures in the field of Egyptian fringe poetry; his writing spans both generations, those of the 1970s and the 1990s. In the seventies he founded two poetry magazines, *Aswat* (Voices) and *Al-Kitabah al-Sawdaa* (Black writing); they introduced fresh and daring writing onto the literary scene in Egypt. In 1993 he founded *Garad* (Locusts), with the aim of introducing a "radical element" into Egyptian poetry. Taha's poetry has also appeared in many official publications, such as *Fusul* (Seasons) and *Al-Qahirah* (Cairo). He has published many poetry collections, the most recent of which is *Imbratureyat Al-Hawa'it* (Empire of walls, 1998).

He has also published many critical articles about various aspects of Egyptian poetry and was recently awarded a government grant to write a book about poetry written under the influence of serious illness. Taha was a member of the group of poets chosen to represent Egypt at the 1999 Arab World Institute Seminar in Paris, France. He is the founder of the Garad Books Series, which has introduced many young poets to the Egyptian literary scene.

A Tale

Nothing separated the bar now from the research papers except for that single, short street, which he crossed to face the shelves all stacked with papers tidied up or bound in volumes.

He thus decided to start with the open Azbekiyah book marché. However decayed, as has recently been claimed, the Azbekiyah park wall remains in the final analysis, the most tolerant book market of all. Approach it with an open mind, and wisdom shall infiltrate your heart, and in time, you shall become a liberal or an ascetic. Side by side on the book shelves lie the direst ideological enemies, and an amicable dialogue is conducted among the various historical times and phases now claimed to be defunct. You will find out, then, that nothing dies but man. You will also see what becomes of paper and book collectors: You will feel secretly envious of those intelligent people who, no longer blinkered, turned the books into a fresh pulp from which colorful paper tissues are made. You will no doubt also reconsider the position of those who hunt down book collectors and place them within walls far different from the Azbekiyah wall.

But the Azbekiyah book market is only the beginning. Alleys and thoroughfares will unfold which, carrying similar names, may be wrongly thought to be similar, though they are as different as heaven and hell.

Venture on foot into some of them and your eyes will goggle, and your mind will falter. Conditions of safety: Shut your eyes, hide your face, and run for it! There are other alleys which you cannot get through unless you keep close enough to the walls and stick to the pavements, appearing as a beggar, which of course you're not. If you are still tempted, you must remember that the ugliest thing a scholar can do is to offer excuses, to find justifications, and to abandon perseverance and fortitude. What you seek now has been sought by many—and their fate remains unknown.

If you pass by a bookshop, get through a street, or cross a square, do not think that you've left the threshold behind and have come close enough to escaping temptation. You must be doubly cautious: there are many bookshops which are in fact traps for the likes of you, especially the ones facing Café Riche. You'll find in them, over and above the interpretations of the thought of the leader-cum-president, many glossy covers, too slippery, from which the steam of hot soup rises. You will have to establish landmarks for yourself, so that you can be sure to avoid any deviation from Suliman Pasha Square—the final destination —except for a necessity permitted by the wise, and previously tried by those in tatters.

If destiny decrees that you get there, and the effect of the nine glasses of liquor is finally worn off, you'll find that your research papers are arranged in the following manner:

(1) Kazantzakis and El-Greco.
(2) Pablo Neruda and the national anthem.
(3) Hassan Hamdan and the colonialist production model.
(4) Guevara and guerilla warfare.

You will find also that the matter is becoming increasingly unclear.

For papers are still papers.
Be more utopian
And less submissive to the martyrs;
Make an indecent exposure
Of these dormant papers,
Marrying words to words
Burning with desire;
Do your best until a fire
Breaks out, and you can hear
Moans and groans
Or until, from among the sounds,
Words emerge.
You must then blow the trumpet—
The trumpet blast of the last day—
So that with the papers upside down,
There will be a resurrection,
Right in front of you,
Of the initial noun
Now past
The uninflected,
The order-giving,
And order-receiving.
Into the fire hurl those
With the big stomachs and those
Who're the smoothest,
Most splendid and exquisite,
The noblest and most correct,
The subject

And object.
Shut the gates of paradise
And hurl down to earth
The most-orphaned words
And recite:
"Guevara and the Peacocks
Hassan Hamdan and Elsa's eyes,
Pablo Neruda and Al-Akhdar Bin Youssef,
Kazantzakis and Cottage Songs."

Then
You could if you would
Go back to the bar,
Shake hands with the next year forcibly,
Or embrace those boys
On the back of whose forearms
No dark feathers grow,
Streets that look not like Shoubra,
And birds that twitter in search
Of a bar or a square,
For a square is a square;
And so
The Egyptians will wander on,
Forget some towns
Stick together,
Get closer
And farther apart.

1991

The Wall of Genesis

One morning a peasant
Woke up and looked about;
He saw no smoke hovering
Over housetops,
Nor a Nile wavering
Over girls' heads.
He heard no woman singing
For her baby retrieved from death,
Nor men who coughed the scent
Of their wives out of their chests;
He saw no tram with a rear full of children
Nor a giggling ghost
On his way back to the graveyard.
So,
He decided that Shoubra
Will precisely be the Shoubra
He had seen in his dream.
And Shoubra came into being.
One other morning
A king woke up and looked about
But saw no curtains veiling his bed,
No flag flying by his window,
No soft thigh between his legs,
No rug covering the weeds
In the water closet;
He could not hear the guards' whispers
Or the rattling of their sabers.
So,
He decided to be the king of Shoubra
Precisely as he had dreamt it.
And the kingdom of Shoubra
Came into being,
With her flag woven of babies' diapers

And ladies' handkerchiefs.

One (yet another) morning
A general woke up and looked about;
He found no moat
About his bed,
No khaki fabric on his body,
No dagger under his pillow.
He found no borders to defend,
No enemies to fight,
No map with contours to follow,
With his baton.
So,
He decided to be the general of Shoubra
Exactly as he had dreamt it,
And the Shoubra military area
Came into being, with Ramses' Statue
Marking the southern border,
And the tramway main station
The northern.
One morning (the last, I promise)
A dictator woke up and looked about;
He found no revolution encumbering
The school bags of school children,
No civil strife claiming the lives
Of café customers,
No traitors who would be executed at your command,
No plot for the media to foil,
No slogan with which to mobilize the masses,
No song to glorify his virility,
So, he decided to be the leader of Shoubra
Precisely as he had dreamt it,
And Shoubra became
The first capital in history
For the third world.

1992

Childhood Wall

1

Because you climbed your bed
Just as you climbed
The roof of an old train
And left it with one leap
Like a paratrooper
Without even rubbing your eyes,
You had a real homeland.

2

Because you washed your face and feet
With one handful of water
And pissed on the heads of beetles
Without wetting your shoes
Which lay between your food and books,
You had a real homeland.

3

Because you had a cat infested with fleas
And a girl friend with hair free of lice,
Gleaming with drops of kerosene,
And a school mistress whose stick
Smelled of your fingers,
You had a real homeland.

4

Because you wore an apron of calico
With two faded ink stains
And several lines crossing on the chest
But most unlike that map
Which you had learned by heart,
You had a real homeland.

5

Because you excelled in hurling stones
On your enemies—both schoolteachers
And the children in the neighboring school—
And stole into the rich man's garden,
Without getting slapped on the nape except once,
You had a real homeland.

6

Because you learned nothing of the Quran
Except the Lord's prayer
And the short "say there's no God but Allah"
And left the congregation at the mosque,
Having scattered the verses on the prayer rug,
Before God found out
That you had not performed
Your ablutions for two weeks,
You had a real homeland.

1990

Anwar Kamel Celebrates
Le Quatorze Juillet*

Don't say that repeated defeats
Have given me that uniform color
Which is indistinct in the dark;
It has always been my color
As it is yours now.
Call it what you will,
But it is all you've got.

———
*July 14: the French Bastille Day.

There's no half death
For you to die;
There's no half color
For me to live;
Therefore,
I shall remain a terrorist,
The way I was born,
Stuffing my head with those dying children
With bloated stomachs
And lying in wait for those blood worms,
like a surfeited spider.
I shall not suck their viscous blood
But will arrange them in my old books
With a spear sunk in the chest of each.
I shall restore their horns,
Now shown round in museum corridors
And their eyes, now stuck to fish heads.
I may also dance around their lined-up bodies
With no shining coffins.
I may even stuff their ribs with my words
Which know neither Rousseau nor Voltaire,
Nor care for the fourteenth of July
Nor look like those three words
Which fall out of book pages
Like aborted three-month-formed fetuses
Sticking to the rear of field guns
Like pubic-hair lice,
But I do celebrate, at every moment,
That shining blade which comes down
Like a diving god to sever the heads
Of kings, harlots, poetry reciters,
Revolutionary intellectuals, generals,
Beautiful women, and men of God,
Throwing the lot in a single basket.
I wish I'd been there!

I could have squeezed myself among
The women watching, peeling their vegetables,
And sat directly behind the basket,
Wetting my quill with that fresh blood
And inditing a love ditty every day
On the head of my sweetheart.

1991

Osama El-Dinasouri

Born in and a resident of Alexandria, El-Dinasouri is classified by critics as an "Eighties poet," belonging to the intermediate stage between 1970s pioneers of prose poetry such as Adonis and the latest wave of 1990s poetry; his poetry belongs more to the latter category. He has published two collections, *Harashef al-Gahm* (Scales of discontent, 1990) and *Mithla Ze'b A'ma* (Like a blind wolf, 1994). He publishes regularly in non-official magazines such as *Al-Kitaba al-Okhra* (Other writings) and *Garad* (Locusts). He writes in both colloquial Egyptian Arabic and MSA; he has also published several short stories.

If I Were a God

I dream all the time of women
Dreaming of me and of female friends
Kissing me innocently,
Embracing me deeply and with the joy
Of wearing a new silken bra.
O my sisters!
Who else but me can you trust
And so recline naked in his presence,
Noisily chewing your gum,
Or sink to sleep, assured that he'll stay up
To take care of your organs
And wash them with his tearful kindness
And whisper his tales to them
To help them grow, unhurried.
You,
My sickly, pale sister,
Take half my blood
And let me bite your lower, fasting lip,

Causing the blood to gush
Perhaps it will be a little swollen.
Let me for once remove, for you,
Your thick spectacles,
And warm your quivering face with my breath
So that, perhaps, the cloud occupying the flabby
Bags under your eyes will be dispelled.
Instead of your finger, let my tongue
Lick your feverish bud
So that the cries of wild cats
Will be heard far and wide.
Perhaps your emaciated body will be rid at last
Of the demons haunting it.
As for you, you house dove
And wise pet,
Allow me to adjust the balance
Of your body's growth,
You, whose lower half has grown
Without the upper half knowing.
I shall undertake hard drills
To liberate your breasts
From the metaphysics of captivity
And rub out with my tongue
Some of the fierceness of your
Savage legs and thighs.
If I were a god,
I would have addressed a strongly worded note
To the god who made you;
I would have much scolded him
For the imbalance of your attractive body.
I would not stop there:
I would even expose him at the gods' forum,
Decisively replying to his miserable attempts
To redress the situation.
Oh, please,

Leave it to me.
I wish I were a god.
I could've melted you once again
With my exhalations,
Changing you into a white malleable pulp,
Spitting my sacred saliva on you,
Amid secret mutterings;
I would've waited long enough
For the fermentation to be complete;
Then, so as to define for my imagination
A solid shape, I would've stabbed you
With my tongue, creating your venerable organ
Which I command to
"Be moist and warm for ever."
I might subsequently let my fancy roam
To visualize the miracle that would be you.
But then I might scream in despair in the end,
Realizing how impossible the whole thing is.
I might feel ashamed of my inability,
Though determined to make a fit apology
For my insolence to God.
The reason is that I would not have found
A more magnificent or perfect image
Than your actual one, but then I might be able
For all this to straighten the slightly arched back,
To rectify the backbone which almost bends
A bit forward, then the thighs!
Oh, the thighs!
I might scrape off two fistfuls
To stuff the slightly flat chest.

1994

Mohamed Metwalli

Born in 1969, Metwalli dropped out of Cairo's Higher Institute for Cinema in 1988 and subsequently graduated from the English Department of Cairo University in 1992. After having his poems published in many and various magazines, he was awarded the Rimbaud Prize for new Egyptian poetry in 1993. In 1994 his first collection, *Hadatha Zata Marra An . . .* (It happened once that . . .) won first prize in the Arab worldwide Yusuf al-Khal poetry competition and was published by the Lebanese Riyad al-Rayes Press. In 1997 he was selected to take part in the International Writers Program held at the University of Iowa. In the same year his second collection, *Al-Qissa allati Yuradidha Al-Nas Huna fil-Meenaa'* (The story people tell here in the harbor), was published by Garad Books. He has also taught Arabic poetry at the University of Chicago's summer Arabic program. He co-founded *Garad* (Locusts) magazine and is a permanent member of its editorial board. He has translated many poems and plays; his work appears regularly in a great many Arabic—and English—language periodicals in Egypt. He writes prose poems in the "new" variety of classical Arabic known as Modern Standard Arabic.

Untitled

> *We are the hollow men*
> *We are the stuffed men*
> *Leaning together,*
> *Headpiece filled with straw.*
> T. S. Eliot

We are two straw dolls,
My friend and I, wearing elegant evening clothes

And shining shoes; his shoes are oval-shaped
And bright like Chaplin's, and my skirt
Is pleated and flowing wide, Dutch style.
My eyes are fixed on his
Most of the time, not to exchange confessions
Of fiery passion or so that I can detect
His drunkenness from the glint in his eyes
When he arrives, tottering, in the small hours,
But because we look better that way
As placed on the piano by the master of the house
With his refined taste and wheelchair.

We on our part repay our debt
By being a credit to him
In front of his friends: as soon as he
winds us up, we
Turn round and round, feigning smiles,
And performing an entertaining dance.
We are not obliged to do this but do it rather
Of our own free will, prompted by a firm faith
In the inevitable division of roles in this world.
My friend, for one, before working
As a dancing doll,
Acted in the theatre, playing now Hamlet, now Christ,
And had played Oedipus, too,
In the heyday of the puppet age.
This is the reason why when the master
Of the house goes to sleep, my friend begins—
Even to this day—to call me by his mother's name,
Sometimes his desire to touch up my breasts
Turns into a craving for a peaceful suckling.
From his eyes, then, flow paper flakes
Which I save for him in return for the protection
He provides later on in the morning.
Role division! How d'you like them apples?

Because we have a golden heart, of pure straw (you can find that out yourself if you cut open our chests), we have a refined straw sense.

This is based on the principle of mutual sympathy, on tolerating and accepting each other the way each one is without insisting on changing the way each is made. It is as far as can be from burdening each other with guilt complexes so tempting to pick up, but which sometimes lead to the creation of barriers which are psychologically comforting for those who pick them up. We avoid applying feminist and Marxist epithets unguardedly to anything. Expressions like "male chauvinist" and "rotten bourgeois" have no actual meaning for us. Otherwise we would be making the same mistake as some of those naive women who turned themselves into the laughing stocks of many generations or as some of the windmill-fighters who conducted their "struggle"—which we, frankly, cannot understand—under a dome of glowing ideas which eventually broke up overhead like summer clouds, leaving them naked and vulnerable to the attacks of those fond of the art of finger-sticking.

Perhaps our political interests are concerned entirely with the conservation of straw resources. This requires a reduction of the amount (tons upon tons) consumed by cattle, sponsoring straw-dependent arts, and following up the progress of space shuttles which break the straw-barrier, for a change.

In short, my friend and I do not care much
For ideas;
We cast them away
Whenever we find them controlling people's lives
Or dominating them.
We turn them round in our heads,
Precisely the way the music turns us round:
We thus perform our dance of destiny
Which we have lately come to love,
As it seems we cannot break out of it,
Singing:
"We are two straw dolls,
My friend and I, wearing

Elegant evening clothes
And shining shoes . . ."

July 15, 1995

This Is How the Magician
Produces a Dove out of the Hat

They are finished with sex,
And the woman, sitting by the fireside,
—Holding the cup of coffee with a quivering hand—
Begins her pious sermon
About the refined manners of noblemen
When wooing the ladies of the Middle Ages,
While her eyes are fixed on the snowflakes
Sliding on the window panes.

◆   ◆   ◆   ◆

Many trains passed through the man's head,
With feet stretched towards the fire, as he
Tried to get a little farther away from the Middle Ages
To see that woman who one winter day
Sat, quite frozen, in front of the fountain
On a public bench in the square,
While a pigeon pecked at her hat
In search of grain.
(He stands by her body in the square, inquiring about her
history or her friends, but his wife leaves them and runs
away in panic.)
He would like to possess her heart
To ask her what she thinks of love
And determine the direction of her feelings.
He would like to talk to her by the fireside.

◆ ◆ ◆ ◆

The woman goes farther afield
In conjuring up the lifestyles of nobility
Until a full skirt grows round her waist,
A huge candelabra comes down
From the ceiling, and a soft waltz
Flows about, filling the room;
Then the man vanishes completely . . .
She finds herself all alone . . .
So, she puts him on the stage
In the final scene of a Greek tragedy
And joins the audience herself . . .
He does not know what to say . . .
So he speaks of the fountain woman
And of her view of love,
Of the hat and the pigeon.
The nobles laugh at him,
So she hates him with all her being—
Moving her eyes away from the window—
To sip the coffee now growing cold.

◆ ◆ ◆ ◆

Suddenly they try sex again
But he—this time—wears an elegant
Nobleman's suit,
And she looks like the fountain woman,
While the cold room is filled to the brim
With candelabras, waltzes, a fountain, snow, a hat,
A pigeon . . . and a flux of happiness.

October 1995

Ali Mansour

An "Eighties poet" and a chemist by profession, Mansour
turned to poetry and has been writing since the early 1980s.

There Is Music Going Down the Stairs

1

The certainty that cheated me,
The certainty that deliberately set up the trap
For a question mark
Predestined to be my companion.
The certainty that surreptitiously
Bespoke common sense:
How to capture peace of mind
And solace.
The certainty that secretly whispered
Determinism, and I was overjoyed,
While water laughed
In the paintings of children.
I caught sight of it
This morning,
Hiding itself, wounded,
Behind some nonsense.

January 2, 1992

2

I did not wrap the evening
With the surgical cotton of adolescence,
Nor promised to give the morning
A high school girl
But I suddenly fell asleep . . .

And saw myself hiding colored tales
In my pocket and tapping the back
Of the empty bench in the garden,
Whilst acknowledging a greeting
For waiting.

January 11, 1992

3

This is a fine morning.
The sun laughs like the dress of a female,
And there is
Music
Going down
The stairs.
And at the fair
There are newspapers, magazines,
And a pay phone.

January 15, 1992

(4)

Therefore take heed of the yearning,
The yearning that grows beside the window.
The yearning that doesn't dry up
In the handkerchief.
The yearning that wakes up
To guard your loveliness.
The yearning that accompanies you
At evening to bed.
The yearning that spoils the pillow.
The yearning whose scent is never lost.
The yearning that gets hold of you
At all times
In my stead.

January 19, 1992

We Must Be Assured That a Fine Poet Will Be Born, Even after Fifteen Years

Pious men
Traveling lightly arrived in town one evening
And had various occupations.
They anointed the head of an orphan,
A little boy, and said "In the name of God."
Some were not bearded;
Some had ideas that smelled of sweet basil.
One smiled and said,
"Take this my boy."
It was neither an orange nor a coin.
Then they came to another city,
Unwearied,
They anointed the head of another orphan,
A little girl, and one said:
"Take this my girl."
It was neither a loaf of bread,
Nor a shirt with two sleeves.
Wait!
Fifteen years.
No one saw the pious men again.
Only the little boy married the little girl,
And people in the morning spoke of strangers
spotted on the outskirts of the city
Who congratulated themselves,
Applauding the triumph.

August 3, 1994

Alaa Khalid

An Alexandrine poet, Khalid is also an amateur film-maker and has several documentaries to his credit. A frequent contributor to *Al-Arba'aeyoun,* he is the editor-in-chief and publisher of *Amkena.*

A Morning Window

Morning.
Me and my things.
Me and the poem I have neglected
On the desk beside the cup of tea
And the box of matches.
Me and the projects I'm thinking of,
Of traveling, making a trip round the world
To hear words for which I expect no end,
Especially to India
To meet the Buddhists and bare my head
Like them, but with my anxiety intact.
Me and the thought of an errand
That I shall run on the seashore
So that low-lying ideas may come
As I walk on, as Nietzsche liked.
Me and a faraway tree
Whose future fruits I can't know,
Nor can I tell what human being
Is hiding behind it.
Perhaps it is the tree deserted by the birds
Because it is bare,
Because it is loyal.

Fall 1993

A Relic

I shall leave you my snores
On the pillow so that you'll enjoy
One scene of my "hereafter."
You may move your head a little farther
From the pillow
Or live independently in another room
Where no harmful sounds, weed-like, grow
Or wake me up, suddenly,
In my nakedness,
With my eyes crowded with the dead
And holding a handful
Of the "hereafter" plants
Like a wreath I would leave
At the grave of sleep.
My snores will grow in the room
Like parasitic plants
And will occupy the ceiling,
While you will survive,
Turning my head, as we do with dice,
In hope you will hit
The winning number of death.

Fall 1993

Aïda

Every day,
She does this duty several times,
Dishwashing,
And with extreme care,
As though lying in wait for any saliva

That may unwittingly
Flow out of the soap's jaws;
She arranges the plates all at once
In one heap over the heart's apron
And, carrying them, walks an
Insignificant distance,
The space between the tables and the chairs,
While comments gather round such spots
Under her eyes as have been formed
By old fossilized tears.
It is as though she's tightrope walking,
Balancing herself to protect
The years she has yet to live
Without a man she'd call her own,
To whom she'd hand over the plates
And who would give her his fingertips.
As she walked on.
She had a vision of the plates
All scattered on the floor;
That all the male customers of the café
Have bent down to heal the wounds
With her joining in;
That with every broken plate,
An idle year of her life went down;
That with every plate she was hit
In her flabby breasts
By little splinters of glass
And by simple eye-shot words
Which would cause the thyroid gland
She carries in her neck,
Like a heart expanding in the air,
To be more sympathetic;
That it would shake the other heart
Like a deserted relic, a moss-overgrown monument.
Their eyes spoke simple words,

But they were good enough
For a woman in her forties,
Who could hold no male saliva
that would deliberately seep through her fingers;
And as it seeps through, she would lay bare
The empty spots in her hands for it to see,
The spots that the soap omitted to get
Between its caustic teeth.
. . . in her forties,
With a heart magnified in the air
And a vein that reveals its hand
Accepting no outspoken feelings,
And with a lonely bottom, a balancing ballast.

1992

Ahmed Yamani

Born in 1970, Yamani is a graduate of Cairo University's Arabic Department. He has been published in several magazines, including *Garad* (Locusts) and *Ibdaa* (Creativity). His first collection, *Shawari' al-Abyad wal-Aswad* (Streets of black and white), published in 1995, caused a furor because of its sexual imagery; in 1998, his second, *Taht Shagarat al-'A'ila* (Under the family tree) was critically acclaimed as mellower and more mature. He writes prose poetry in Modern Standard Arabic and currently occupies the post of assistant editor in *Al-Qahirah* (Cairo) magazine.

Streets of Black and White

The light went out in the Cairo skies.
A blind man crashed into the railing
On the metal bridge and was stained
By the wet green paint.
The paint is invisible in the dark,
But he feels the wet paint on his skin
And falls into the Nile.
Two cars ran over me;
One was going in the wrong direction.
I was caught in between them,
And the blood did not gush out of my head.
I am right here under the cars
In a little house surrounding my ribs.
An ant jumps out all of a sudden
And bites my right arm, and I groan.
Water hoses extinguish the fire of the two cars.
The fire is dark gray.
The water hits me, but no one sees me,

Which is much better.
I emerge from under the wheels,
Wearing my dinner jacket
And on my way to the old Cairo Opera House.
My Rolls Royce is washed by the rain;
The music is boisterous this night,
And I need to dance with a pale-faced girl.
I drive towards Claude Bey Street,
But leave the car and take
A donkey-drawn cart
On Abul-Ela Bridge,
Carrying a group of women
On their way to visit the Cairo cemetery.
I rest my head on the thigh of one of them,
Sleep, and wake up wet.
The police are chasing me in a student demonstration,
I run to hide under the two cars,
Without bleeding this time either.
The two cars disappeared in a large pit.
I jump after them
And land in a huge funeral procession,
I salute everybody and laugh.
A man who doesn't like me binds my right hand
With a chain which he passes
To the mourners one after another.
The dead man's hearse ran quickly to the grave.
The shroud merchant, the nurse, the tomb guard
And his family, the dead man's children,
And the neighbors, all pose in a commemorative photo
In honor of the dear departed,
With me in front, in a white *galabia*,*
Holding the camera.
The man leaves the chain to cry.

---

*Loose one-piece dress-like traditional garment worn by men and women.

The cigarette falls off from my lips
Onto the carpet, and the procession goes up in flames.
I run away,
Carrying my child on my back.
He was weeping alone.
The child does not stop crying;
I press his forehead, and he stops.
I press again, and he cries again.
The child's eyes are shining bright,
And his face bespeaks a single agitation,
Unchanging, for four hours.
He falls off my back as I run
And catches fire after a simple explosion.
Am I passing through these farms
For the first time, leaving behind a murder?
Who will burn up my finger prints
Or flood these fields after me?
The dead child occupies a vast land area;
His blue eyes lie
Thirty meters away from the explosion point;
His black shoes are hung from a tree.
His metal hand swims slowly;
No blood comes out of his head.
Will you send us a new coloring kit
So that we may color his eyes, tongue, and lips,
And raise him up as a flag flying over the fields?
As the night seems clear
And the moon about to give full light,
A caravan of camels passes by.
I hang on to the rear,
And at a distant cafe
Unknown to me, I take a seat.
Twenty teaspoons turn round
In the cups all at once,
But no other noises at all.

A woman comes in with her eyes
Fixed directly on my organ.
I start to take off my clothes
In front of everybody;
We groan together
In an exposed corner of the café.
The woman goes out, never to reappear in the dark.
It must be that the power cut,
The uncertainty that candles are available
To us at all times,
The heat whose source is unknown,
The unimportant spectacles of my friends,
The roads where the inhabitants are locked in,
And the windows that are no longer visible,
Must have helped the words
To pass over our heads as we talked for hours
Until our throats grew dry.
The words that come out
Without us heeding their weaving—
The vigorous words which we exchange for hours
Until the door is suddenly opened,
Or two cars collide in the street,
Or the water tap creaks,
One drop falling after another,
And the rhythm sends us to sleep.

1992

Aliyah Abdul-Salaam

A "Nineties poet" and free spirit, born in the conservative city of Mansoura, Aliyah later moved to Cairo in search of a less traditional, more bohemian lifestyle. Having lived in Germany for a while, she sought political asylum in South Africa but was deported. Her time is currently divided between Cairo, Sinai, and the Red Sea.

In Front of the House

You licked the dust that covered their antiques;
You watched your neighbor carrying her caged bird,
Followed by the little girls carrying lit candles
On their way home.
The construction worker,
A young head of a family,
Had actually sunk into sleep
On one of the three beds
Without taking off his shoes.
In front of their houses, you'll feel within
A vague passion growing for the plants
Floating on the surface
Of the pool of tears you've created
As a statement of the depth of your feeling
Of alienation from them.
In front of their houses, you'll feel
That you're a lover of humanity
And your existence is great.

December 1992

The Mermaid

My heart was petrified;
Then I went down in the wetness
To new friends. I was in pain.
I almost broke up, like any stone in the roadway,
Into fragments, so that I would be sifted
And scattered in the recesses of the sky above
In silent beauty without a tongue.
Now I reside in all things;
Sometimes I follow the chickens
On their way to the factories
And increase the quota of water
Allocated to the plants
Inside my home
And feel overjoyed with the rain
Coming down.
I reside in the land
Like mountains on seashores,
Which are populated, sometimes, with human beings.

December 1992

A Bird Close to Old Houses

Close to the old houses
There's a rotten air
And a weakness,
And both cover the dreams.
There, too, lives luck
Which I put up in a small pyramid
To let it occupy a concrete space
In the vacancy of the world,
The world that craves to be devoured,

To be completely devoured;
An eye that looks, an eye that shakes off sleep,
An eye that cannot see.
People in the city love rain,
But they try not to get their clothes wet.
Also
They prevent children from playing around the trees
Because they see in the dark horizon
Two birds and a ladder.
One bird hovers near the light,
The other perching on the ladder.

February 1993

A Village Near a Church

This garment with the thin white stripes,
I bought from a textile shop
Near a church of average beauty.
Yet it surpassed my dreams
And all the beauty I had imagined.
It was itself the church that
I had dreamed contained
A secret I had to capture.
I paid the price of the garment,
While glancing at the church
As though resisting a great aversion to myself.
It is quite hot near the shore,
The sky is overhead, the sun is hot, without fire,
The clouds are gray, in splendor,
Blue the color of water,
Sun light is white, like a vacancy.
The village inhabitants, short,
In harmony with life and nature,

Evoke in my soul intimations of harmony
And familiarity.
It happened now that I, a lonely girl,
Put on that garment itself
And craved to face an undeceiving mirror.
Why doesn't it happen now
That my self could sit before me
Like that old chair
Visited by people having different
Languages and cultures?

February 1993

Yasser Abdullatif

Born in 1970, Abdullatif graduated from the philosophy department of Cairo University and now works in the Cultural Program of the English-language Nile TV. His poems have been published in many magazines. His first collection, *Nas wa Ahgar* (People and rocks) was self-published in 1995, and since then he has gone on to publish a number of successful collections.

Archeology

1

Alternating tiles of white and black
Make up the floor of the hall,
Safely touched by the domestic slippers,
To the study.
An old wooden desk,
With a surface of rough green leather
Traversed by the fingers, turning over the papers,
Unconscious of the texture.
The flood-lit door opens onto the garden,
A minute staircase, two or three steps,
And a broom of straw abandoned on the threshold.
A short palm tree is the entire legacy
Of the garden, with spaces of worn-out lawn
Here and there.

2

Miraculously a desert springs up here.
When twelve lean cows die,
And a row of palm trees grows,
A provincial university is established,
With a paved road running by it,

Wide enough for a man wearing an old fez
To walk alone, enjoying the warmth of wisdom.
With the hot, dusty Khamasin* winds blowing,
He considers the aesthetics of death:
The drunken throes may persist for decades
Before the thinkers take them up
And weave them into a theory of life

3

The dances by the sea,
The female bodies washed with beer and lemon juice.
With my face to the sea, I turned my back on them
Smoking.
Their music does not accord with the horizon;
Even in picnics death is present
For us to contemplate,
All of us, each in his own way.

4

We are leaving the houses
In search of a postponed death,
For the tales of death out of doors
Are more numerous than the tales of death indoors.
The houses which we had thought were
Matchboxes for sleep, sex, and reading—
Actions that help us break the limits of place—
Only existed to be transcended:
They do not, in fact, exist.

5

There is an old house on a historical street to which
I am related by something like regret;
I stand on the pavement opposite,

---

*A fifty-day (*Khamsin* means "fifty") period of dust-laden winds that herald
the coming of spring in Egypt.

Looking at the wall panels, the windows,
And the surviving decorations:
A clothesline that witnessed generation after generation
Of clothes, and the fingers that played on the pegs
The tune of social climbing.
There is a house which, if I had once inhabited it,
I would not have seen the way I see it now—
Like a homeland and a friend; a house
Only exists when missed.

6

I shall go out to the desert like a fugitive,
And under the skull-smelting sun
My past life will melt away,
And I shall see my future as a mirage.
Two girls trying to get some water for their father
From a well with a wall of clay.
I shall escort them on the way back home,
Watching the light of the setting sun
Play on their silken dresses,
One blue, the other wine-colored—
Two color spots in the sea of sand.
Two slits in the dresses, opening
And closing, reveal their Bedouin legs.
Their old father will talk to me
In metaphysics, give me the younger one's hand
In marriage—the one with the small feet—
But I shall secretly sleep with the older.
For ten years I shall shepherd his flocks
And know the taste of pastoral love.
For ten years, then I shall return to the city,
Carrying the vastness of the desert
In my breast and worthy
To break the law which
I ran away from.

1994

Bahaa Awwad

Born in 1969, Awwad graduated from Cairo University's Faculty of Mass Communication in 1992. He was one of the first poets to write prose poetry in Egyptian colloquial Arabic. He has been published in official publications such as *Kitabaat Gadida* (New writings) and *Al-Qahirah* (Cairo) as well as such unofficial magazines as *Garad* (Locusts) and *Al-Kitaba al-Okhra* (Other writings). His first collection of poems, *Shams el-Aseel* (Afternoon sun), was published by Garad Books in 1998.

Declining Sun

The Use of Remembering

A young man of twenty-five, a paper and a pen, and an attempt to put the last five years into language. All words are odd and queer, and the years have accumulated with astonishing spontaneity. Four girls are being deflowered in a festive ritual, and a fifth, a few steps away, is wiping off with an eraser the traces of a chance touch to her hand by a boy on the bus. There is a strange similarity between the features of the last five years in the face of the young man and the features of the five girls, as if the entire scene were photographed in a sudden, candid shot with a surprise flash.

The Use of Naming

Nizar Qabbani's poem, the one entitled "Bread, Hashish and the Moon," is one of those that deeply moved me. The only thing that drew my attention to it was the title. I have therefore decided that the title of my poem will be "Declining Sun," for reasons quite peculiar to me.

Names and titles have an independent logic, a predestined one. Otherwise what difference can there be in the scales of the spirit between two girls who have left the same impression on the chart of experience, one called "Iman," the other "Hayam"?

The Use of Astonishment

Twenty fingers intertwined with power, tension, and shadeless soft lighting; two birds mutually bleeding on the first steps of pleasure; four lips touching and separating in a savage dance with music from the tradition of anarchy; and a mass of flesh, homogeneous and red-hot—all remind me at a quick romantic moment of the first questions, the ones that have lost their luster, though their answers remain like economic tables, accurate and well-organized.

The Use of Sex

Assailed by despair, with the years continuing to accumulate with the same lethal rhythm, I remember that throughout the years that have elapsed, there has been a boy within me fighting against unknown forces. Sometimes he hid himself from them; sometimes he appeared unarmed, though armed only with his naughtiness—an innate impetuous naughtiness.

Whenever I am assailed by despair, I remember the hiding boy and wait impatiently for his thrilling performances, surprises, and vague reckless acts.

The Use of Friendship

A boy and a girl defy nature: suddenly they are capable of ignoring the hormone-governing laws. A homogeneous tissue— they need many things for the tissue to remain homogeneous. Perhaps tomorrow everything will change, and the savagery of chemistry, with its direct effect on the soul, may come into play. Perhaps we shall exchange a surprise kiss, after a nervous desire for candor, to unburden the spirit. The anarchy of fate may land us in a tight trap as a married couple for all to see—very happy in front of people. So many things may happen in the future in spite of ourselves or, perhaps, because we want them to happen. As for today, how nice it is for us to be friends. Just friends.

The Use of Colors

Blue, green, red, yellow.

There is in this world a living language.

What is meant by living is that each symbol within reflects a whole world; and as the symbols interact, life deepens, ramifies, and is now in harmony, now in discord. Without them, life will lose the insipid idea of its first origin.

The Use of Romanticism

Do not cite the holy books whatever the subject you deal with in this world. Beware of citing the holy books! Always remember that within you is an area of pristine simplicity which always can, if sincerely approached, give you pure wisdom.

The Use of Rest

Visited by hope, I look upon the years with courage, unterrified by their accumulation and stable rhythm. Once again I am ecstatic with wonder and capable of enjoying even loneliness. I rest my head, unworried, on something and wait in peace of mind. It is a moment of thinking of nothing—of thinking of nothing at all.

1996

Youssef Rakha

A journalist, writer, and poet, Rakha is currently on the staff of *Al-Ahram Weekly*'s culture page. He began publishing poetry at a very early age, and he is the youngest contributor to *Garad* magazine to date.

Dust Storm

The Dust Storm

On this day my city was struck by a dust storm—while I was in the street—and I could not light the cigarette. I looked at the sky as it heaped the dust on me and at the thin, lean match which shared my sorrows and looked at me apologetically.

The Woman Sitting Before Me

This woman sitting before me.

With her body, her mind, and the hair falling down her shoulders, she reminds me of my beloved and my mother—of Thursday nights and Friday evenings and hot meals on tables.

I could no longer look at her as an ordinary person. She carries in her body her mind and the hair falling down her shoulders, those Thursday nights and Friday evenings.

And the hot meals on the tables.

The City

"This night I burned up a hundred cigarettes." Yes, I no longer
   know any meaning for life.
"By day, when the sun gets too hot,
I like to walk in the streets."
The fruit-seller pushes his cart wearily.
"I could not catch the bus."
You shouldn't smoke too much,

You'll get sick—"The bus was too fast."
You shouldn't substitute darkness for light.
"But I wanted to meet the city."
The night was not so lonesome.
What's that in his hand—another cigarette!
"When I arrived at the big building,
I had to climb up the stairs."
The city's become already overcrowded but . . .
"This night the sky was in total darkness."
I know you're sad, I know that very well.
"This night you burned up a hundred cigarettes."
The night was not so lonesome.
"But I wanted to meet the city."

1996

Youssri Hassaan

Born in Cairo in 1964, Hassaan graduated from Ain Shams University's History Department and is now editor of the culture section of *Horiyaty* (My freedom) magazine. He is also an editor for the cultural section of *Al-Masaa* (Evening) newspaper. He is a member of the Supreme Cultural Council Selection Committee for the *Al-Kitab Al-Awal* (First books) series. As well as poetry, he has published and presented a great many papers on colloquial Arabic poetry and the relationship between culture and the mass media. His poems have been published in many periodicals including *Adab wa Naqd* (Literature and criticism), *Al-Shi'r* (Poetry), *Al-Thaqafa al-Gadida* (New culture) and *Akhbar al-Adab* (Literary news). His first collection, *Qabl Nihayat al-Mashhad* (Before the scene is over) was published in 1996 by the Cultural Palaces Organization. His second collection, *Saba' Khataya* (Seven sins) is currently under publication.

I Considered Myself

There
In any obscure corner
You'll find me standing.
I can dance well
When I switch off the floor lights,
Flirt with the girl in the opposite building
Through the slit in the window shutter,
And write passionate love letters for my friends.
—What were the reasons for the French Expedition
to Egypt? An easy and quite ordinary question.

All mothers look like my mother,
All houses look like our house,
All school-children are wearing cotton aprons,
And nearly all are carrying canvas bags.
But I'm sure that if asked the same question
A hundred times, I wouldn't know how to answer it.
But how?
I left my desk at the bottom of the classroom,
And walked up to the blackboard—took me ages!
The entire population of Rode El-Farag
Had opened their windows and watched me,
Winking to one another.
I had to get out of that fix quickly.
I remembered what my grandmother once said:
I considered myself a camel.
I shouldn't, therefore, make love to my wife
In public; that was, too, why I decided
To stand in the rear
At the morning school parade.
Yesterday I dreamed of being at a big party
Where two singers competed with me.
I had learned a lot of traditional
Country lyrics and knew how to sing them beautifully.
Once on the stage, however, I wished
I could wake up quickly
To get out of that embarrassing situation.
In 1973, a fellow schoolboy used to write
Colloquial verses every day; he recited them
Over the school loudspeaker, getting
A huge ovation at the end.
My verses were much better than his, or
So was I told by the colleagues
Who had, in private, heard my verses
Which my elder brother had written for me.

During my last attempt to swim in the sea
Last summer, a friend of mine lent me
His face to go into the water with,
But my new face surprised me,
Was soaked, and disintegrated,
And all the beach people came round to look
And whisper mocking remarks.
I had to get out of the fix as soon
As possible.

January 20, 1993

Magdy El-Gabry

Influenced by his background in folklore studies, Al-Gabry wrote in the Egyptian vernacular. Born in 1961, he studied at a traditional school for learning the Koran. After graduating from the Institute for Agricultural Studies in 1983, he went on to get an master of arts from the Higher Institute of Folkloric Art, and later on occupied editorial positions for the General Egyptian Book Organization's Young Library series and for *Theater Horizons Magazine*. His first collection, *Aghostos* (August, 1990) and his second *Bizabt wa Ka'innu Hasal* (Just as if it happened, 1994) were self-published; his third, *'Ayyel bi-Yestaad el-Hawadeet* (A kid chasing stories) was published by the Cultural Palaces Organization in 1995. He died of cancer in May 1999.

A Child Hunting Tales

I was about five years old, and Gamal Abdul-Nasser could lift a whole building, standing up, with one finger. He wasn't like my father, who, when he went into the bathroom, produced a sound that I clearly heard, while clinging to my grandmother. She told me the tale of Sitt al-Husn* and how she tricked the ogre with a dummy, an exact replica of herself made of sweets, which she put in her own bed. The dummy sat up in bed exactly opposite the keyhole in the door. When the ogre charged, my granny protruded her chin to mimic the ogre's voice, while a yellowish white saliva line came down from her mouth. I laughed secretly for fear that my father might hear me and realize I had not fallen asleep. If he did, he would go out to work in the morning without getting me my favorite breakfast *belilah*,** or giving me my pocket money, or letting me help him wrap the bandages round his leg.

---

*"Lady of Beauty": fairytale princess common in children's stories.
**Cracked wheat with milk, a kind of porridge.

My hair is left to grow, with a distinct part right in the middle and with a chili pepper tied to the lock falling down my face. A wooden door had been fixed to the staircase entrance with a bolt too high up for me to reach. When my grandfather went out to buy something from a shop, he took me along, holding my hand. Once, while he let my hand go to light a cigarette, I bolted away.

My grandfather is still waiting for me to fall down so as to help me rise, brush the dust off my clothes, take me by the hand back home.

While the children and I roasted a dead duck or while we caught the wasps in the waste ground behind the mosque, tales were told and jokes cracked about the things that happened in their homes or in the homes of their neighbors. They laughed, and sometimes I joined in the laughter, but I could never tell any amusing story. I was once put in a corner: if I didn't tell them something, I would be barred from their games. I then made up a story with my grandfather as hero. Once, I said, he was asleep under a mango tree in the garden when a rustle was heard overhead. He rose to find a thief in the top of the tree, carrying a sack, and shouted at him. As the thief tried to get up, his underpants came down. My grandfather got some chaff which he scattered round the thief in a circle, which became his prison; then my grandfather went back to sleep. When he woke up, the thief was where he had been. "Have you learned your lesson?" my grandfather asked. "You won't come here ever again, will you?" "I won't, ever," said the thief, whereupon my grandfather removed part of the chaff circle with his foot, creating an opening, and said, "Off you go, then!" The thief put one foot out, then the other, and, assured that he had left the circle, pulled his underpants up and put the sack on his back and flew away.

Naturally no one laughed. I, too, stopped laughing thereafter at any joke or anecdote told by the children. The repetition of the incident made me feel I had grown up and stopped playing with them. It was then that I saw the mosque. I went in. I learned by heart three parts of the Quran (out of thirty). Sometimes I played teacher, and made the boys recite the chapters they had learned by rote before me or led the night prayers as "Imam" when the real master-cum-Imam was away. Since then I've come to be known as "master," though I still feel frightened when my grand-mother protrudes her chin, still hate to wake up too late to miss the *belilah* or the pocket money, the penny I would add to the other pennies previously saved so that I could buy in the end a real leather briefcase and a pair of shoes with fine rubber soles.

His apron was not pressed, either by being put under the pillow nor, of course, with the hand iron. At the meal break he blushed as he got out the two sandwiches—one with egg and pastrami, the other with luncheon meat—inviting me to share his lunch. When the schoolmistress asked him to recite the "fisherman rhyme" and he couldn't, I was amazed.

I was afraid she might ask me lest I should fail, too, though I knew it by heart and could even write it all down without making a single mistake.

I sat under the flagpole. The school was empty. I had taken off my shoes and put them beside the school bag. My eyes followed a flock of white doves on the wing, while a bite of the *ta'miyah* sandwich was still being slowly chewed. Suddenly the dove leading the flock came down, perched right before me, and said, "Get up! Your father is dead."

I laughed and leaped out of my dream. I found my mother sitting on the sofa, crying. "Is it true, mother," I asked, "that my father is dead?" She jumped to her feet, put on her black *galabia,* snatched her head scarf, and flew to hospital with me following, barefoot and with unwashed eyes. I looked overhead to find the white doves flying slightly ahead of us. Running, so as to keep pace with my mother, I said, "You know, it was the first dove, you see, that told me." My mother dragged me by the hand without responding or even looking overhead. I walked on, stumbling, while with the other hand I rubbed my eyes and looked at the doves and at my mother. I was afraid lest death be something nasty that made my mother cry, lest it be something known only to the white doves which I see every day when I go to sleep alone after performing my rites of ablution and after finishing my school homework and the homework of the Quran-teaching school and which I now see flying over, and ahead of us. In the morning I did not go to school, and the house was full of people, men and women screaming; there were lamentations, dress-tearing, pouring of water and eau de Cologne, white sheets, and a green quilt over a coffin; the men fought over who would carry it, and the women tried to prevent it from leaving the house. I could not go to sleep after the night prayer and stayed up until dawn. I prayed to God never to see the flock of white doves ever again when I was alone in bed. Since then I never look overhead whenever I walk alone. I still cannot love doves, the color white, sleeping alone, or sleeping early.

After you die. The milk spilt on the ground will be gathered in the aluminum pot and will be put on top of the head of the woman who passed suddenly in front of the bike ridden for the first time by a child trying to play hooky during the break.

The silver tray will be quenched by the six silver glasses which suddenly glistened on the fall of the water, beside the sycamore tree underneath which lay the holy tomb of your Saint Multifarious.

Schoolmistress Samia will continue to ask us to explain the meaning of "angler" and "lascivious," holding in her right hand the pencil with the eraser and in her left hand the tale of the Brave Tortoise which she had recounted yesterday before we left. In the morning, when we line up to sing the national anthem, a tall boy will be standing uneasily at the front, and the fourth file will be minus one boy. By the time the physical training teacher has devised a means of adjusting the files, I will have found a trick to suppress the laugh that insists on breaking the grave mood fit for writing about my own death.

1994

Mohamed Lasheen

Born in 1971, Lasheen graduated from the Arabic Language Department of Cairo's Ain Shams University, where he also directed several plays. His poetry first appeared in *Garad* (Locusts) in 1996, and he is a familiar figure on the Egyptian Literary Fringe scene. His huge size has earned him the affectionate appellation "the Sumo wrestler."

Nearly Three Million Years Ago

Within my bosom a man has lived for nearly three million years. He has a thick beard, his body is all covered with hair, and he has nothing on except that bit of tiger hide over his genitals. He loves raw liver with coconut juice and resides in a small cave with no swimming pool. (He keeps a little dinosaur, which he calls "Kaka," with immense experience in dancing the cha-cha and in frightening the girls in the neighborhood with his penis that is a little over two meters in length). The man has a cudgel used in driving off his insipid friends and a granite bed capable of withstanding the tremors of his body. He makes love to five of the female gender—the penis-eating type—in the missionary position.

It happened once that a woman inquired of him about an address, but finding that he liked her, he removed her garments and dragged her by the hair to his cave. Why not? It happens, too, that if he's overcome by a sudden desire to scratch his bottom while crossing a public square, he will lay bare his lower half completely, and would not hesitate to belch in the face of his sweetheart at their very first meeting.

Within my bosom is a man who lived nearly three million years ago. He thinks that the sky is a huge plastic bag containing the rain, the birds, the clouds and what have you; that this bag enwraps the earth at the time of lovemaking so that it produces people, trees, and caves; and that the sea is the semen of the sky. In spite of all this, he loves children very much, likes their green feces; indeed, he collects it in small bottles as souvenirs. He makes a seminal point of keeping silent all the time, thinking that speech, any kind of speech, is absurd clattering. He is a refined man indeed, but uncultured. He is not eager, therefore, to cultivate any interest in himself. He only implants many eyes into the carbuncles of his foot, leaves his organs in places he cannot remember, mixes his saliva with his blood to find out what sort of mixture will be produced, then tastes it, swearing that it needs a little more salt.

He has lately been to a dentist with a strange complaint: his testicles had calcified and merged into one. The dentist advised him to use a regular toothbrush instead of the broom which had destroyed his gums.

A noteworthy postscript: some Bedouins claim that they saw him, inasmuch as anyone can, soaring in the sky with two red gloves and two wings made of tin, and that he uttered incomprehensible words. The precise date of the sighting was the second of December 1972 A.D.

1995

Nightmares Fit to Arouse Misgivings

Since rheumatic fever and obesity destroyed
My joints, I have been stuck
With a glue of pungent piss odor
To my steadfast bed.
I experience the world from a small aperture in the floor where
    extant and extinct kinds of insects gather.
Sometimes I watch their festival of storing provisions and,
    occasionally, their mating under my magnifying glass.
(I laugh to no end when I imagine the amount of semen
    produced by the male.)

Sometimes I examine a strange ritual
When with their bodies they make intersecting circles.
Bored, I pour a glass of water
On their world.
A Noah may be born into the world,
Building his ark from a biscuit crumb
And so would save them from the deluge.
But the deluge spares no one.
One day I woke up from a terrible
Nightmare.
There was a huge beetle, followed by three young ones, rolling a
    ball of dung. I believe it could have gotten it from my own
    bowl under the bed and was making straight for my head to
    judge by the direction in which his antennae pointed. With a
    speed I never thought I possessed, I hurled my shoe at it. His
    entrails grossly soiled the place as if I had killed a calf.
When I later learned that this beetle was the very sacred scarab
    of you, I was overcome by a fit of crying—very deep indeed.

1995

Eman Mersaal

A prolific writer, Mersaal has three collections to her credit and has been published in various magazines such as *Gerad* and *Adab wa Naqd* (Literature and criticism). With a master of arts in Arabic literature, she started writing in the 1980s. She currently resides in the United States.

Neutrality

I shall empty my hand
Of all the sedative lies
And burn before his eyes
The clay which he had molded
To the dimensions of his dreams.
He will point to the left side of his chest,
And I shall nod with the neutrality of nurses.
He would like to believe, before the coronary coma
Is over, that his death wish
Will not conceal the family rifts.

1992

Repetition

Unusually the window panes are tinted gray;
Awe-inspiringly huge,
They allow the bed-ridden
To observe the traffic
And the weather outside the building.
Usually the doctors have sharp noses
And glass spectacles

Which establish a definite distance
Between them and pain.
Usually the visiting relations leave roses at room entrances,
Asking forgiveness of their future dead.
Usually there are ladies with no make-up
Who walk on the square tiles,
And sons who stand under electric lamps
Embracing the X-ray files,
And confirming that cruelty may be condoned
If only their fathers had more time.
Usually everything is repeated,
And the pigeonholes are filled with new bodies,
As though there's a punctured lung
Inhaling all the world's oxygen
And leaving all these chests
Out of breath.

1992

Too Many Times

Too many times
The doctor came into our house
To say, "You're too late."
That is the reason why
I whisper the medical history of loved ones
Who are not buried when they die
And open my room's windows
The minute they are tightly shut.
I have a mourning of my own
When the music of neighboring wedding parties
Rings loud.

1992

A Portrait

His heart, synchronized with my steps,
Was not enough,
Except as a memory, as an intimate
And bad smell.
Perhaps he hated my summer trousers
And the music-free poetry,
But I caught him more than once
Getting dizzy with the noises of my friends
And ecstatic with the smoke they left behind.

1993

Mas'oud Shouman

Born in 1966, Shouman writes in colloquial Egyptian Arabic and specializes in both poetry and folklore. He is a member of the prestigious Itihad al-Kutab al-Masriyeen (Egyptian Literary Association) and Gamiyat al-Fannaneen wal-Udabaa (Artists and Writers Society). He is editor of several literary series including Kitab al-Thaqafa al-Gadida (New Culture Books), Kitab al-Udabaa (Writers Books), Zakirat Al-Kitaba (Memory of Writing), and Tizkari (Commemorative). He has also been assistant editor of the *Ibn Arous Egyptian Arabic Poetry Magazine* since 1993. In addition, he has published numerous studies on folklore. His collection *Awal Prova—Diwan el-Fatafeet* (Fragments, first draft) was published by the Cultural Palaces Organization in 1996. He has two new poetry collections currently under publication: *Rigly At'al min Sanat Sab'a w'Sitteen* (My legs are heavier than 1967) and a book of poems for children, *Al 'Asfour al-Akhdar* (The green bird).

A Dance with Nothing On, with Nobody Around

This is the point where I shall stick my arrow,
Go out in the dark and stretch my hands,
And do my dance; I haven't decided
What it will be like, but I shall say to it
"You're my dance! I have recognized you just now
By the smell of my perspiration
And my panting up the stairs."
(There was a little girl with me, with long braids of hair.)
I shall wear my cap and hold my crutch . . .
Wave it in the face of rust-devoured nails.

(Incidentally, a large drawing paper was stuck
On the classroom's salt-eroded wall,
Where dead birds were painted,
And fixed with nails.)
—These are my shoes.
—Yes.
Their color is odd, and the lace trails
On the floor.
This is my plaster face which I took off.
In the afternoon. I've put it on the broken chair;
Perhaps someone will find it and give it
To the junk dealer.
Perhaps it will appeal to the lady who wears
Thick glasses, and so she might add it
To the antiques she's kept since 1930.
I shall perform a mad dance
For the first time:
It has no numbered movements,
Nor is it calculated, till the end.
I shall dance it alone,
Or to the drunken crowd in any bar
I've never visited, as much as the drops of beer
Remaining in their glasses will allow me.
This is the turban I have inherited
From my grandfather—it's in a cesspool.
This is my moustache which is said
To have made me a spitting image of my father.
I shall chop it off and have a close shave around it.
This is a very old rosary—thirty-three beads.
No, not ninety-nine,
One a pearl, another a ruby, a third emerald.
This is my share of my dead grandmother's box.
I shall scatter the beads in different towns
To give each the chance of a blessing.
And these are my clothes.

I shall dance for the first time
With nothing on and with nobody around.
It may be dark.
It may be humid.
But this is the point where I shall
Stick my arrow.

Winter 1992

Shehata El-Iryaan

Writing in the vernacular and an Eighties poet, El-Iryaan is also an acclaimed novelist. His latest novel, *Dekka Khashabeya Tasa' Ithnayn bel-Kad* (A wooden bench barely big enough for two) was awarded the very prestigious 2001 State Incentive Award.

Thermometer of Happiness

In rhythmic beat I respond to the tune of that song, having forgotten the words; and with a voice my ear cannot hear, I only hum the opening and supply any words for the runaway lyric.

Even the tune is beginning to run away. Fragments of thought clash in my mind. The radio blares in the fruit-juice shop, with the volume turned up sky-high.

Why am I not happy?

I've had a shower, a shave, and some coffee; besides I am meeting some friends with whom I haven't spent an evening for some time.

I'm supposed to be happy.

That is why I don't feel that my happiness is enough.

How do you calculate it?

One can measure the degree of one's happiness. One can have, say, a happiness thermometer. When the reading is 42 degrees Celsius, one is dead. At that reading, one may be feverish enough to scorch or to embrace whomever one meets in the street—a young girl, someone in love, an old man, a foreigner, a child.

It doesn't matter. The main thing is to bow courteously and say:

—I'm happy. My happiness is 42°C and could help you: sympathy? information? ideas?

Surely everyone needs something. I, for one, would like to measure the degree of my happiness and have always had serious doubts about it: I don't think it ever reached 42°C.

There's always a little anxiety at a distant spot in my nervous system.

A vague anxiety: this joy, I fear, will turn into sorrow.

That is why I've now decided not to take the bus.

It's happened before, only too often.

As soon as you get onto the bus, someone steps on your foot, or . . .

I really don't know what I am doing.

I now have happiness, snippets of a song tune, and am humming to myself in the street.

I've had a shower and a shave.

A girl with beautiful eyes, coming in my direction, looked straight into my eyes, at a distance of two meters, and as she passed by, I said "Good Evening" in a startled voice.

She didn't hear me.

I think I never said anything.

My voice never left me: I heard the raucous echoes in my ears, repeated for another two meters. To get rid of it I screamed: "Good Evening."

Someone answered me, "And good evening to you, too!" laughing. I laughed back in awkwardness.

April 1997

Ihab Khalifa

A graduate of the Arabic Department of Zagazig University (class of 1997), Khalifa writes prose poetry in Modern Standard Arabic . His poems were first published in *Al-Khitab al-Hamishi* (Marginal discourse). His first collection, *Akthar Marahan Mimma Tazun,* (Funnier than you think), was published by Al-Kitaba al-Okhra Books in 1998.

No Need to Discourage Dreams

The women are returning
From the People's Assembly
With frustrated souls.
Their request to have the roads
Slope-paved has been rejected;
So was the request to persuade
Shop owners to install VHF loudspeakers
Playing songs that praise the women's beauty.
Nor could they get permission
To have special small trolleys made
On which to roll
The butane gas containers home.
They will surely get over
Such disappointment; and
There was no need for their dreams
To be discouraged.
They will shortly visit the gas depot,
Each will paint her face
With attractive colors
And wear a numbered card,
Having written the family name

On the container.
They would never concede defeat and retreat
But will write to CNN
To help advocate for their cause
With a publicity stunt
And invite a sufficient
Number of referees.
The first friendly match will be held
Tomorrow: the referees will decide
Which one of them came home first,
Which one could carry the gas container
And still manage to "walk in beauty."
The clever one indeed will be the one
Who could perfect the art of high-heel prancing
And so get home with her high heels unbroken.
At the Sydney 2000 Olympics,
Egyptian women will be prominent
As players who have obtained a patent
For inventing the game of the numbered
container and dangerous fuel.
As of tomorrow, the children will arrange
A special diet for their mothers
So that the XXL training suit
can be replaced with an M size.
Our objective is to have our mothers
regain their slim figures
To pass this crisis
And put an end to flabbiness.

July 1997

Guirguis Shoukry

Active in many fields, Shoukry currently occupies the post of theater critic for the *Radio & Television* magazine. He started writing poetry in the early 1990s. He has been published in many magazines including *Garad, Adab wa Naqd, Ibdaa,* and *Al-Kitaba al-Okhra.*

A Personal Portrait

I establish relations of familiarity
With all things, believing that each one
Should possess certain things
To love as a homeland.
One should undertake daily rituals
With things before discarding them
And should train oneself to accept loss.
I know, on the other hand, that things
"Never die but fade away."
Sometimes I grow my beard, have a dog,
And visit certain streets.
There, at the end of space,
There's my café, my mother's house,
The joy of my colored crayons
As I yawn in front of my books.
All this often happens when I lose my things,
One morning, perhaps a different warning,
And try to change the world.
Also,
I'm a man who goes to the bar
In the morning, sits in subdued light,
Smokes, has a drink,
And asks the waiter:

"Why do I establish relationships with things
Then lose them, even as a homeland, too?"
He will smile in his turn, lighting
Another candle, then advise me
To take the "time factor" into account.
He will then withdraw from the scene,
To traverse the whole of eternal time
On the table, whilst I remain
Happy with my hatred for the sun
And raise another glass to my lips,
Drinking to the health of a morning
Which deceives us and
Which we lose every morning.

June 1997

A Good Man Talking to Himself

1

I am a camera,
A large store of memories.
I register everything
But understand nothing.
I have recorded wars
Until my memory turned
Into a gunpowder depot.
I now forget the image of my loved ones
In my cup of coffee.
I talk to myself and tell things
About old countries
Which had inhabited this air,
Then passed away like music,
About people who carry their animals and houses

Every morning,
Asking the sea to keep an eye on them,
Who often fall out of their coats,
Making a vacuum in the air.
I find it enough to bite a woman's lip
Every evening
While we take off our pants,
Ordering our organs to work in silence
So that the scene is not shaken.
I speak to myself again.
I am a camera.
All my shots are illusory and empty,
And my roll of film is overexposed
To laughter and burned out.

2

So, this man became a good man
Who kept a smile under his pillow
And went to bed knowing
There would be no revolutions to lose in the morning,
An animal who flicked his ears
And spoke to himself.
That is how I felt ashamed
Of women groping in my pants,
And I grew an age older in one night
Without my mother knowing,
And learned fear.
That is how I felt ashamed of God
At every funeral
And hated the deceased,
And at every history lesson,
I bit my nails and saw my father
Dead on the blackboard.
Do not believe me, for I am a good man
Who loses a whole "planet earth"

In his cup of coffee every morning.
This is not a human being.
This is "injury time" shared by the crowd.
The result of adding up all the moments
Spent at each scene
Is a long life and dead living.

3

"Do you love me?"
"You know that I do," she said.
So, this is a repeated scene.
Yesterday's food on the table is cold,
On its way to the dustbin in protest,
And I talk to myself about a fear
That lies in my bed,
Weeping or smiling
Like a fighter confusing his defeats
With his playing cards
Then counting how much laughter
He's got left.
"Do you love me?"
"You know that I do."
This is, then, my corpse leaping
To its shirt, and they argue.
The picture is in a poor state
Where language learns depravity
And the drunken man believes that philosophy
Is the trade of the Gods and the craft
Of his forefathers, then forgets
The face of his beloved in the mirror
And opens his door to the night
To come back a little shorter
And in colored garments.
"Do you love me?"
This time, the third, she vanished

Like a soft-lit image,
And he knew that he gave his loved ones
Sleep but stayed up himself,
Talking to himself
About a good man like a camera.

September 1997

Meelaad Zakaria Youssef

Funnily enough, Youssef is now a sports columnist. He
writes a regular football column in *Al-Fursaan* (Knights)
sporting magazine.

The Sadder Man

Why do all his women die
Before he is fully in love with them?
That was what the old sacristan
Asked himself on Sundays
While filling the incense burner with coal
And watching the swaying incense
In the middle of the altar.
He is as surprised by the portraits of saints as
With their penetrating eyes.
They catch him stealing a look
From behind the altar curtain
At the faces of little girls
With the tresses sneaking to peep from
Under the white scarves.
No one saw him
Sitting at dawn last Sunday,
Baking the Eucharist bread in the old oven,
And taking regular gulps from the bottle
Of holy wine which the priest
Hides in the altar cellar.
How cold his nights were
As he walked in his white robes
Among the empty pews
And imagined crowds of veiled girls
With narrow eyes flying about him

And filling his verse with tears.
As his little daughter with her pink veil
Swayed, holding the rope,
Of the old copper bell
And flocks of angels
Danced around her,
He got the church columns together,
Embraced them and rained kisses on them.
He chased the white doves,
Raising his eyes to the minaret;
Then his dove-daughter came down to him and
Sat on his knees, and he undid
Her braids
And read to her the nine o'clock prayer:
"Love is as strong as death my daughter.
Your death is as strong as love, my daughter."
. . . . . .
The dove flies away,
Leaving behind
A piece of myrrh in his mouth,
A golden cross around his neck,
And a warm body on the altar.
The old sacristan goes up,
With a flock of veiled girls behind him,
Towards the statue of crucified Jesus.
Quietly,
They put on his head a wreath of thorns,
Bring down the statue,
Raise the old sacristan
Onto the cross, and
Fix his hands and feet with nails
While a white dove stabs his chest
So that he instantly bleeds
Both blood and water.
She gives him a drink of vinegar,

Feeds him her wing,
And quickly disappears.
With eyes lifted to heaven he says
"O Father! How cruel you are! O father!"

February 1995

Sadiq Sharshar

Sharshar writes in the vernacular. Originally trained as a lawyer, he works for the Ministry of Culture for the Mass Culture Program, which aims at providing cultural facilities for remote and underprivileged sectors of Egypt. He was first published in *Garad* and is a "Nineties poet." He has many collections in print, sponsored by the Ministry of Culture. His work has appeared in many publications including *Al-Qahirah* and *Adab wa Naqd*.

Charlie Chaplin

Full house tonight at the Kit-Kat Cinema,
Charlie Chaplin is here, checking the tickets.
Hurry up!
See who's at the gate handing out laughter.
Someone is screaming at two lovers
In the back row.
The kiss is already on the screen!
Charlie Chaplin got out of a wardrobe,
Twirling his cane;
Spotting me, he smiled and put on airs.
At the door of the room he took his leave of me,
As though the road was a horse
In metamorphosis,
A fantastic scene of a roving circus;
Who was it you greeted?
Those enamored of sorrow,
And I bowed down.
How long did I walk,
And how long did it take to get back?
At the door of the silent movies,
I left both coat and hat.

Your shadow on the screen
Is drawing the sorrows of the audience.
How many hankies have you got
In your pockets, if a sparrow flies away?
Your dreams are at large in the streets,
Of people who go to bed at sunset
While you keep roving
And changing in color.
To the door of the wound you come back
In the small hours, drunk;
How many sad persons have you
Greeted with broken accents?
Your teeth fell out
When you laughed
And ran after your smoke.
The windows, your eyes, were far away.
You extended his hands to find
That your hands were a street turning.
I took you in my arms and wept.
I saluted.
And disappeared

January 29, 1996

The Singer

This is a scene where a singer
With both hands amputated
Plays the accordion every day
Beside the garden wall.
"Do you remember me?"
"Not quite."
"Did you catch him?"
"Not exactly."
He appeared in the square for a minute

Then disappeared.
The smoke of car exhaust
Gathers the thoughts of the craftsmen
On their way to the factories
And of the intellectuals dozing
In bars who do not hear his voice
Swept away with cigarette ends and sawdust.
He was,
Whilst the music accompanying him faded out,
The only singer,
And I was the only member of the audience
Surviving from the lute-playing years,
A string . . . but the road "key" is lost.
As we crossed is the pavement,
He cried on my shoulder.
In the impoverished bar we drank.
The years forgive the dead who can't keep count.
He scribbled on the table his journey
Through the city.
Day was coming back
When I remembered his song.
The music scale came out of his pocket
And the gypsies emerging in the glass light
With the two windows open to the moon, and
Fardous sprightly hopping between the tabors
And the fire.
He remembered her.
He remembered her silver ankle bracelets,
And his eyes gleamed, traveling between
Her palms and the flames.
When she laughed, revealing her two gold teeth,
He was entranced.
He had in his pocket a lock of her hair
And a mirror made of mountain sands.

June 20, 1997

Safaa Fathi

Born in the Egyptian province of Minya, Fathi moved constantly around Egypt because of her father's job in the Egyptian police force. She finally emigrated to Paris, which has been her home since 1981 and where she completed her Ph.D. on "Brecht and Edward Bond: Contemporary English Theater." Her many collections of poetry are published by Sharqiyat Press. As well as poetry in Arabic, she writes plays and theater and film criticism in French. Her latest publication was a play on terrorism; Jacques Derrida wrote the introduction. She has also directed two documentary films in English and French.

For Heiner Muller

To Heiner Muller

Poem 1

Uneasy poetry looking for an alternative
The first poem is an elegy
Written in typescript the day I saw your ghost
When your grave contained no bones
. . . . .
Waiting for the bus
I had a wash in the tombs of intellectuals
I ran, naked, down the road lived with whispers
I sprinkled literary prayers on the slumbering souls
And muttered
In just a quarter of an hour

Author's note: Heiner Muller (1929–1995) was a dramatist and poet from East Germany, who passed away over a year ago.

I shall embrace the statues
That lay down in your heart
· · · · ·
The sirens of emergency vehicles carry
To the residents here
A passage where the stones are depressed
And where in its details dance
Ravens carrying crowns of violable mould
· · · · ·
It's now five past four
The afternoon of an October day
And I should then hurry up
To catch the sail of your shroud flying on the horse
No
I have another five minutes
Which I shall leave to you
Time enough to climb that old tree
And throw down to me a tongue
With which I can talk.

Berlin
October 1995

Poem 2

We [they, now] protect autumn from a cough of a man suffering
   from truth cancer. In the garden I waited for some flesh that
   was not dead, and at the café I waited—vague like them—it
   is Berlin—it is the theatres—and the time twelve, an October
   midday, and the place the Berliner Ensemble Theater—the
   relics of the skulls of Brecht and others.
We in return for women's images
At a table, the café of Selim al-Hawwas
And you
Too many typographical errors

Because you worshipped cancer
Cancer of the breast in the Hamlet machine,
Cancer of love in the quartet,
Cancer of the throat when you deserted
The shadow under the wall.
When the players left to
Put on some of the conventional costumes,
Wishing you would utter a single word,
Oh, then the seats fell silent
In the actors' suitcases—
The beginning of the outcast dialogue
When "space" fled the city
And some "time" was dissolved with the boiling water
And the show was over in the numerous harbors
Before a group of living languages
And wires which you carry
Always with you.
Narration has eyes with fugitive dreams
Because you do not write novels
You said
Beauty lies in the smoke of the ending
And the same tales groan on the secret police desks
Of the postage stamps
You, Heiner Muller, the writer who disdained
To go out onto the balconies
And left me to imagine the chandeliers
That bore the palm
And eavesdrop
On the only black jacket
That you left on the coat hanger
At a wall which always bled
With raindrops

Berlin
October 1996

Poem 3

That's the way it is, he said.
We shall never meet except through the dust.
In his all-deceiving death
They got together for a cup of coffee,
But I didn't see his memory.
There was a mix-up of events.
I went back. No, I didn't go back
To breathe the coal dust
And the taste of dark bread.
In Paris, there among those who didn't know him,
I declared—Oh, hail to the month of August—
I would be going to Berlin.
My face glimpsed the shocks
In its mills.
There were mirrors reflecting her image:
In its sins lurked the temptation of old childhood.
Still,
I was shocked to hear the young voices:
"In a few moments we shall share the world!"
Words
Poured by the writer onto paper the minute
The Berlin Wall fell down.
Time for the airplanes . . .
I get ready to look for my memories
In the nooks and crannies of the city.

Berlin
October 1996

Don Quixote and the Flour Mills

Poems seeking the image of the sense storm
Raised by Don Quixote, the hero
Of the air that I cannot breathe
Quite happily. He floats on high
In the flayed imagination
And the tremor of dreams.
When the eyes at the café began to turn white,
I heard a hoarse sound; was it the raucous
Echo of the obscene insults?
When the ovens burned with aircraft noises,
I had in the grave little children
Whom I bore one day, being an old maid,
When I hummed a funereal tune
So that God might dream of me.
I took off my breasts
Because they do not write songs
Nor worship the ancient caretaker of the inn.
I shall remember one day that I shall live
In the hymns; that
I killed my name several times
During the celebrations of the birthdays
Of Muslim saints, that you're still
That same boy of times past
Who gave me eyes that ran after the ice;
That we do not play with pots and pans
And fear the lamps;
That I do not hate everybody;
That I lose my voice, gradually,
With the approach of spring;
That you are fighting the air;
And that I am sand.

Cairo
February 18, 1997

To Don Quixote, crucified in the heart
Of Tahrir Square, resurrected
At the top of Palace Square, El-Minya.
(Or was it the other way round?)
The sheikh buried in flour

I knocked at the door of Revolution.
He said,
"I love you." I didn't ask.
With them I set about writing leaflets
Flirting with the messages I buried
Inside dates—impossible fruit!—
And passed them through prison gates.
Then
I screamed behind the walls,
Practiced suicide,
But I didn't die
Because I have seven lives
Or nine, like Plath's cats,
On whose skin shining worms grow.
That is why I wallowed in flour,
Was dressed in white
So as to drive the mills away
Like Sleeping Beauty in a Harem palace.
I got myself ready for vanishing
When at dawn the soldiers came
To talk to the old woman,
When the pistols galloped in mid-morning,
Laden with their sweet-sounding bullets.
A meek guard took my arm.
Where are the cats, I asked, and where
Have the games and cafés gone?
"Go away," they said, perhaps to play.
So the years became dressed in black
And went round the graves in search of

A bed
Or young words
Or a speech from whose twists and turns
Storms came down, the storms of beards
Wearing the veil of an anarchic sunlight.
That is how my blind minds came to acquire
The stuff that may give birth also
To some migrating birds.
Let us dance together round the totem of lunacy.
Let us pour out the words of the orators
As exhalations on the harbingers of spring
Let us embrace the years, in the arms of the Seine,
Or the Nile,
Burying our hair in the flood
Now stained with white,
In the ecstasy of the speeches
Aflame with the romanticism of the fog.
Here are the relics of a heart that
Did not depart in time.
Today is
Faraway in the moisture of cafés,
But close to the threshold of pale complexions,
Hoarse-sounding amidst the tunes
Of the vocal cords of my years wallowing
In the dreamy flour—
I do not care for them on the regular occasions
Because I haven't lost my memory.

Cairo and Paris
May 19, 1997

Haytham El-Shawwaf

An Alexandrine who later settled in Cairo, El-Shawwaf was born in 1967. Working in the unlikely field of catering, he has nevertheless published several prose poems in colloquial Egyptian Arabic in official periodicals such as *Al-Qahirah* (Cairo) and unofficial ones such as *Garad* (Locusts). His poetry is characterized by its casual, chatty tone which few others can match. His first collection, *Ascenseur* (Elevator) was published by Garad Books in 1998.

Half a Lemon, Half a Cigarette, and Half a Desire to Have It Off

Knowledge falls down, and slogans fall down; nothing remains except two human beings—only two—who bear each other some rancor, a few memories, ranging from happiness to pain; and a couple of tears going down their cheeks for no reason.

1. Showikar

That's the name of the fat girl whom I loved simply because she shared my desk in class. I never tried to kiss her, or even to pinch her cheek. She's fatter now. Having had so many children, she's no longer willing, I imagine, to start any new relationship, not even with me.

2. Ikhlas

"My love!" she said, laughing, and I felt I wanted to run fast. Now I think I could have beaten the fastest sprinter, Forrest Gump . . . So much so, in fact, I was afraid lest my uncle should be jealous of me, if he noticed my confusion—and my mouth, wide open in a silly smile—and tell her.

3. Mona

Her tales in the old house built of mud bricks dealt with necrophilia and how it had a flavor all its own. I remember once finding her naked and how I saw her in the bathroom with bare breasts. All this could've helped me to talk to her in words that looked like her breasts. But when she slept with me in the same bed, I felt nailed down to my place and could not release a word. When someone came into the room, I pretended I had been used to this. In a manner that appeared perfectly normal, I dealt with her as a sister.

4. A Handful of Girls

The handful of girls who aroused me in my masturbation three or four times a day—well—there's nothing between us today except half a lemon, half a cigarette, and half a desire to have it off; there is the feeling of the increasing similarity between me and a full basin in which a number of things are sinking—sex, love, honest feelings and dishonest feelings, and the various cultures. Every two minutes, one of them tries to resist drowning and raises its head a little, but then another thing, bobbing, gets on top of it. It is probably because of this that nothing is left between me and any other person except half a lemon, half a cigarette, half a desire to have it off, and a string of words broken in the middle.

Summer 1996

The Devil's Symbol

Suddenly while shaving, you looked in the mirror to discover that your canine teeth have grown remarkably long. Getting closer to the mirror for a confirmation, you discovered for the second time on the same day that your head is adorned by two ivory horns which are exceedingly beautiful.

In fact, you now hardly need to look behind, or extend an arm, to discover the existence of an arrow-tipped tail or indeed to look round for the three-pronged spear, the diabolic symbol, for surely you'll be needing to use it from now on. Oh, I can see you now with the most wicked smile on your lips as in your mind's eye you see the faces of your friends! Meeting you after the transformation, not a single one of them would be able to provoke you or even to utter the least embarrassing word, knowing full well that he or she would thus be opening the door wide to evil which you must love dearly! Like every other genuine devil, you'll know how to take this and start playing games with him, or her!

Summer 1996

Imad Fouad

Imad Fouad was born in 1974. His first collection of poems, *Shadows Hurt by the Light,* was published by Al-Kitaba al-Okhra Books. His second, *The Retirement of an Old Don Juan,* has just been published by Sharqiyat Press.

Truth: I Have Five Fingers on Each Hand!

The bus I just got off of
Which I have regularly taken for five long years,
Twice a day,
The same bus that pours into my chest toxic exhaust,
I have just gotten off of, with a leap—
Sudden and calculated.
Only when I go to bed do I feel those
Sharp needles in my tongue;
Only mother knows: smoke is not the only reason
For this cough.
Oh, the cough!
An artery always swells at my crotch
All around the abdomen when I cough.
I feel I have been filthy for a week.
If I put my five fingers to my chest
And scratch,
My fingernails emerge blackened and greasy.
My life will be short, I know;
Throughout my childhood,
I often deceived the old shopkeeper
At the haberdasher's by stealing anything
I could lay my little hands on.
I kept stealing with persistent earnestness.
The fingers which will blacken and grow greasy,

The fingers that transferred the merchandise
Of the senile old buffer to my school bag,
Are the same fingers which were bitten by my cousin
When he discovered my new game.
He scolded me, warned me I'd be found out.
He first threatened me: "I'll tell your mother
If you don't stop," but I was sure: "You can't!"
I am an incorrigible liar!
His fingers, training to pull the trigger,
Grew red on my cheek and patted me,
The fool!
How could he believe my blush
And retract his suspicions!?
My fingers are small
And grow bluish in the cold;
When I slipped them in the pocket
Of his woolen *galabia,*
I scratched the smooth banknote
With its embossed designs.
I fished out a new twenty-pound note.
It was easy.
Only my heart beat fast
And my joints shook for a couple of seconds!
It's the same emptiness; the space
Between the bathroom window
And its wooden frame
Will make me end my bath with a sudden quiver
And get out, trembling, and wet
And pull on, with my fine fingers, my clothes.
My fingers still keep growing with a patience
That I can neither glimpse nor see
With the same deep marks and print lines,
The same shy perspiration in the palms
Of strangers and new friends.

December 1997

94   *IMAD FOUAD*

Maher Sabry

After graduating from Cairo University's English Department in 1993, Sabry rebelled against working in his father's chemical factory and began to publish his poetry in such official magazines as *Ibdaa* (Creativity), *Al-Qahirah* (Cairo), and *Fusul* (Seasons). He also co-founded *Garad* (Locusts) and published poems there. His poems have been translated in such English-language periodicals as *Cairo Times* and *Middle East Times*. His collection *Marionette,* for which he also did the artwork, was published by Garad Books in 1998. Sabry also works in the field of graphic arts; he designed the Garad Books logo and has just published an illustrated guide to Egyptian feminism. He is also very active on the Egyptian Fringe theater scene and recently founded his own theater company, which presented the play *The Harem,* based on the poem in this anthology, at the 1998 Cairo International Festival for Experimental Theater. In 2001 Sabry became involved in the field of gay activism and was forced to move to the United States.

The Harem

She must look at her face until she grows to hate it,
Paint her lips and eyes,
And, with glass fingers, consecrate her body
To diamonds and pearls, then exude
An exciting perfume, as she waits for the Sultan . . .
(Sometimes she looks out of the window
At the handsome gate-keeper.
He visits her, in her dreams
And dances with her a tango.)
To the ticking of her Swiss watch,

She makes her usual rounds
Of the women's quarters
Just to break the boredom,
Hunting for whispers behind the closed doors.
—Usually the pretty ones are slandered
More than the others—
She may stumble upon a passionate moan
And so may steal a look from behind
The curtain, hardly shocked by the sight
Of a breast dangling in the mouth
Of a loving woman or the sexual games
Of two slave girls.
(Nor does she care that one is being
Unfaithful, in her mind, to the other.)
In the bathroom, the slave girls
Wear nothing at all except their skin—
Having stamped them with the seals of Christian Dior
And Fabergé—and steal
The conversations of the eunuchs about
Battles fought with sword and RPJ—
Marj Dabiq, Hiroshima, Vietnam,
Then scrabble after the latest fashions and
the secrets of late-night seductions.
(She has
To fill her ear to the brim
Without leaving the backstage of slander.)
When she leaves the basin of water,
The eunuchs' secrets scatter out of her hair in droplets.
Her buttocks shake under the gaze of aged eyes,
And the slave-dealer, an ugly old woman, smiles,
The rosary beads running through her fingers.
(Usually she does not mention the name of God:
She has to arrange for a private meeting
For two lovers in return for kisses
On the slave girl's body and a bribe of embraces.)

At night
The newborn moon reminds her
That it is her turn
To spin an embryo for the king.
She lets him dye her with his sweat
And distracts herself from his absorption in her body
By looking at the patterns on the wall.
She closes her eyes
And masturbates alien dreams.

1998

Troy

Once upon a time
A wooden horse burped,
Regurgitating the soldiers in his stomach,
Armed to the teeth,
(Behind a purple commander).
They opened the walls up
And sketched the end on the gates of Troy.

In a dark corner of the horse's entrails, ,
A single warrior remained.
He sat alone,
Holding a sword and a piece of sweetmeat
And dreamed of the Athenian,
The lyre player, who did his hair in ringlets
And who painted columns for him, one Ionic
And another Corinthian;
And who, in the nights of entertainments and festivals
Smiled only to him
From the back row in the theater
As they watched . . . a modern tragedy.

He wished then that he had a telephone
To tell the lyre player how much he missed him

He put his head out to look
Outside the wooden frame
And was snatched up by the night and the full moon.
He went down to the arena
And walked, unsteadily,
With a heart beating fast and trembling.
He raised his sword in the face
Of a young Trojan man, fleeing;
Each suspected and feared the other
And as the sword holder loved life,
He let the deserter run away
Outside the walls.

At their parting
The lyre player had reminded him of his duty as a fighter
To Ares and Zeus, of his duty
As an Athenian to his homeland.
The warrior had smiled sarcastically,
Ridiculed the gods of Mount Olympus
That shed so much blood . . .
Then he took him to the temple
And at the feet of Aphrodite
They made love

He wished then that he had an airplane
To fly to the lyre player

He threw down both sword and helmet,
And resting against a dilapidated wall,
He recalled his winter memories—
The stage of the sea and the balcony.

On the beach,
They stood in the embrace of massive cliffs,
As they together repeated the marriage vow
Before an imaginary altar.
They let the vast sea be their priest,
So huge and strong and merging
Into the sky: the sea hurled his waves
On the rocks with a splash, spraying
Their bodies with foam.
In the evening,
They shut the balcony doors,
Slipped under the warm covers
In the dark room—all dark
Except for a little box that told visible tales,
Radiating a faint light
That showed him his lover's face.

He wished then that the lyre player could watch television
To follow the news of the battle

The screams, the obscenity, and
the mutilated bodies horrified him.
He woke up to find himself still
in a corner in the entrails of the toy,
While the soldiers, with iron-clad chests
and bare thighs, were still praying
to the gods, waiting for battle.

He wished then that the wooden horse had stayed
Outside the city walls.

1998

Marionette

You must
Drive your car
Down an unlit road
And ignore the phosphorescent eyes
Which persistently blink at you.
You must count from one to a hundred,
To hundreds,
Then stop at one thousand and one
To pick a few kisses
And apply the theories of embracing.
Do not cry if your sweetheart left you
On the evening of your birthday;
For all lovers, behind the strings, depart.
Perhaps you cannot get away
From the traps of family duties . . .
And so you spin the cobwebs into tethers
That weigh heavily on your conscience
But cannot move your fingers
Lest you should break them.
At a table at Groppi's,
You may pour your feelings
Into your girl's glass,
To unveil to her the strings
That paint your images.
Then, her silly dreams will be exposed to you,
And with unintentional cruelty,
You will make her a gift of a teenage god
(Which she wished to put in the microwave oven
To mature a little).
In a lightning visit
You insert your first letter in her hand
—With a childish smile—
Then leave her for your date with the desert.

There, behind the sand dunes
You'll find a strange, turbulent world:
Dozens of rats
Carrying sacks full of fear
And lizards suffering from hallucinations . . .
They will exchange looks with you
And laugh hysterically at
Your camouflage jacket
And your boots . . .
Then they will ridicule with sharp boos
Your rifle, filled with chocolates,
With which you chase the gnats
And the dusty night moths.
Perhaps you're more fortunate than
The scarecrow: You can hurl your
jacket up in the air, take off your shoes
To play in the sand with your toes
—Which will not arouse anybody's disgust—
Then stare at your shadow striding before you
(Taller and more graceful) . . .
You could count the years of your life,
To exchange them for a few basic remarks,
Or to thread them onto one of your many strings.
Why don't you bury some of them
In the sand,
Then spend the rest of the evening
In writing letters, which you'll quickly
Regard as junk?
On coming back again,
You'll find that your girl
Has also failed
In removing the threads from her body
To use in patching up her torn identity . . .
Open the front door of your car for her
And grant her the right of citizenship

To acquire her nationality from the seat beside you.
You must—this time—drive your car
On a road without any lighting
At all

1995

Fathi Abdullah

Abdullah is the editor of the General Egyptian Book Organization's New Writings series, as well as assistant editor of *Al-Qahirah* (Cairo) magazine. He graduated from Dar al-Ulum, Egypt's oldest college for language and theology in 1982 and has been writing poetry since the 1980s. His latest collection, *Sa'ada Mota'akhera* (Late happiness) was published in 1998.

On the Declaration of Joy

1

I may be a boxer
Who lost his wife
And does not admit it to his friends
But loads his pistol
And goes out for a walk
Like a cowboy
Who could not sleep alone
In a spacious room,
So he joined two priests
In short robes
In their declaration of joy
And to become a hero he must,
From now on, kill his mother.

2

The scene: a black woman
With bare breasts
Prompting the tanks to kill
The peasants
Who have pledged

To engage in sex
At a public festival
And to designate
Ballet dances
As the last dwelling for a hunter
Whose prey has escaped,
Or else make do with looking at
The lenses
And carrying the dead to the back
Of the shed.
For we may find a goat which
We used to describe in wars gone by
As a teacher
Placing before us fresh maize
And verses from the Quran
Which we might require
In sleep
Or to protect our children
From war.
We have not as yet realized
That what we possess
Is not fit for annihilation
Except once.

1997

Small Bodies That Cannot Be Heeded

In what happened, nothing
Was planned by anyone—
By any of those
Who came down:
They all died in the same way
For the train passenger

Who sat in front of them
Did not fold up the newspaper
Or burst out laughing:
Did the hooded men take him
At Christmas time,
Leaving two bottles
In the fridge?
His wife did not believe
That the bodies of his sons
Were stolen by the doctors.
And when he held his breath
During the visit,
He did not tell his elder sister
And found animals pulling down
The house walls.
He must find a new flat
On whose door to hang
The silver ankle bracelets of his mother
And some of the bodies
Left behind by the train whistle.

1997

Hoda Hussein

A graduate of the French department of Cairo University's Faculty of Arts, Hussein is very prolific for her age. She has translated numerous books from French into Arabic: novels, poetry, and other books. She has also published many collections including *Leyakun* (Let it be so) and *'Ashwa'eya* (Randomness). She also represented Egypt at the 1999 Arab World Institute Poetry Festival in France.

I Can Talk to Them

I close my eye on its red haze
And the hallucinations of light and shade,
A glaring desert distributing its heat,
A strip of hot vapor touching the ground
From which come out sheep and a staff,
And a pale girl grinding her teeth
Arouses the sand with a pastoral song
To the alternating clicks of her shoe heels.
Her hair flies about, black and curly,
In defiance,
With the regular beat.
She is an image that will vanish
The minute it takes shape;
A little relaxation is enough
For the carpet to be pulled away
From under our feet, declaring
The formation of other images
More stimulating to the sense of amusement.
I shall not be quite dead:
I shall only shrug off from my head
A depressing memory.
I make up an insult

And call it my future life,
Then hurl it onto their bottoms.
I am immersed in reading and translation.
I seek diversion, too,
In listening to the different accents
Of the cats at night, ranging from
Hunger to fear to courting—
Things that remind you that you're still alive
And that also bring some gratification to the soul.
Something holds your attention:
A square mirror with the sun right in focus
It is not quite square.
You see a sun with rims
Digging shacks in the corners of your eyes
When you shut them
To make it easy for the sun
To scratch them out with fingernail-tips.
There are images carried by the heat
To your eyelids: three black trunks,
With threadbare flesh;
Three women extending their
Umbilical cords in a tangle
Tight enough to swallow you up;
A huge beetle, revealing her teeth,
Lustfully calling while she looks after
The little worms in the spaces in between them.
I shall exchange my room
For another one full of junk
Caught in nets of moss oozing with slime;
And with wide open eyes I shall see
How I shall run into soft bodies
Flying about in the copper-colored water
Of the room, and in my head.
A slow-motion tape records the dialogues,
Which turn to intermittent yawns.
My friends will visit me to look

How my flesh is now sponge-like in the water,
How my fingernails have come to be soft.
They will look for the protective charm
Which I may have taken off here or there,
And they will sink deeper,
Sucked in by the water,
And I shall watch them
With my eyes, thrown by the termites
In the bottom of the room
When the seaweed will tickle their bodies
Which gradually surrender until
They float in silence,
Horrified,
And then
I can talk to them.
But I, as is typical of the dying,
Am overcome by a desire to make a confession
And to take a few last photographs
Of my friends' features.
I remember that I cough and spit.
My stomach is mercilessly grinding the food
And churns it out as outcast as a leper;
I am filled with wrath to the brim
And am very happy to peer into the faces
Which had suffered much in explaining
The concept of happiness.
A memory I shall miss
Just as someone loses the taste
Of the earliest foods, with the falling out
Of one's sharp-pointed teeth
Without knowing why
And with a silly joy
Imitates the smile of mother
Sticking her hand between his jaws
To take out as many of them as she could

Before hurling them to the sun.
I shut my bloodshot eyes
And watch the full scene:
A girl in the empty space
Swinging from a pendulum hanging
From the sky, from an unknown source,
Asks the passers-by what time it is,
And the departure time of the train
Bound for her father's grave.
There's no one, unfortunately, there
For her to be at his beck and call.
She, welcoming, subdues her nature;
She bends within, like a concave mirror;
She could not be otherwise,
And collapses, sometimes,
For him.
A girl is hanging from the ropes of the square.
She cuts her hair and scatters it round
With the scarlet flowers
And latrine-smelling handkerchiefs
On the approaching cars.
She hides a defect in her feet,
Spinning merry humorous yarns about it;
Then she rushes
Before the yellow city lights
Fall on her face.
A picture fixed on the wall of the room,
An angry girl is examining
What her end has turned out into;
She advances further,
Removing from the branches
Their yellow intertwined leaves;
She vigorously shakes the trunks
And makes a sound like howling.

December 1994